Counseling for Medication-Assisted Recovery:

A Practitioner's Guide
Second Edition

Gary Blanchard, MA, LADC1

© 2014 by Gary Blanchard

All rights reserved. No part or portion of this book may be reproduced without the express, written permission of the author.

ISBN 978-1495441103
LCCN 2014902844

Also by Gary Blanchard:

How to Build and Maintain Recovery

Positive Path Recovery

www.garyblanchard.net

Positive Path Books
West Brookfield, MA

Table Of Contents

Chapter	Page
Preface to the Second Edition	7
The Changing Face Of Addiction Treatment	9
A History of Medication and Addiction Treatment	11
The Challenges of Medication Assisted Recovery	21
Client/Counselor Readiness for Treatment	29
Creating Connections	33
Motivating Change	37
Self Awareness and Connection	51
Cognitive/Behavioral Techniques in MAR	61
Communication Skills For Recovery	73
A Positive Approach to Relapse Prevention	85
The Transitioning Process	95
Medications For Mental Health	99
Marijuana and Medication Assisted Recovery	103
Closing Thoughts	105
The Eight Principles of Positive Path Recovery	107
Guided Visualization for Connecting to the True Self	113
Redefining and Restoring the True Self	115
Relationships	116
Identifying and Overcoming Recovery Barriers	117
Bibliography	121
Other Resources	127

"Those who cannot change their minds cannot change anything."

— George Bernard Shaw

Preface to the Second Edition

I am not the biggest fan of updates to books. As an adjunct professor, my students often complain that updated editions make it impossible to resell their old textbooks. There are times, however, when some changes should be made; I have come to the conclusion that this is the time that this book needed to be updated.

Over time, I have come to think that some points in the book could have been stated more clearly; I have taken this opportunity to do that. I also felt that it was important to explore the history of using medications in the treatment of addiction in order to better understand current attitudes and beliefs about medication assisted recovery. That chapter also offers some basic information about medications that are currently used in treating addiction. That list is subject to change and is not meant to be comprehensive.

The changes in attitudes toward marijuana use, both legally and by some treatment programs, also bore some attention. Lastly, I wanted to add some resources that I feel would be useful for those who are working in the Field.

I hope this book will help you better understand MAR, and to be the best clinician you can be.

Chapter One:
The Changing Face of Addiction Treatment

For many years treatment of addictive disorders has been provided by addiction professionals in sites dedicated to addiction treatment. Medication may have been used to assist in detoxification, but treatment was generally a drug-free process. The ultimate goal of most treatment tends to be total abstinence from all mood-altering chemicals. The use of self-help groups, such as Alcoholics Anonymous (AA) and Narcotics Anonymous (NA) is highly encouraged, if not mandated.

Until recently, the one exception to this has been methadone maintenance programs. This approach differs primarily by using a medication, methadone, to help the client maintain their physical desire for opiates, while providing counseling to help them make the cognitive and behavioral changes needed for recovery. The programs are staffed by addiction professionals in dedicated treatment facilities, there is still a focus on total abstinence from all other mood-altering substances, and participation in NA is encouraged, even though many people in the NA program disapprove of this form of treatment.

With the recent introduction of medications like Suboxone for opiate dependence and now Campral and Vivitrol for alcohol dependence, treatment has begun to shift from dedicated addiction treatment facilities to the physician's office. This shift presents new challenges to addiction treatment professionals.

In the following chapters, I hope to address these challenges, while offering a series of tools and tips to help addiction professionals learn to adapt to the changes in the field and to be effective in helping clients achieve success in their recovery. The information comes from both study and practical experience.

As I stated earlier, the world of medication-assisted recovery (MAR) is constantly changing; any details offered on current medications will quickly become obsolete. Though I present an overview of current medications, I highly recommend that treatment professionals follow the latest information from magazines, journals, and other sources to keep up to date with the latest discoveries and details. This book will focus on the main work of addiction counseling professionals, providing the skills that people need to be successful in recovery.

Chapter Two:
A History of Medication and Addiction Treatment

The current attitude toward medication assisted recovery may be hard to undserstand, but it is based on a long history of misguided or perhaps fraudulant attempts to treat addiction throughout history. In this chapter I will give a brief overview of the history of medication for addiction treatment and a general look at medications that are currently used in addiction treatment. For a more in-depth look at the history of addiction treatment, I highly recommend *Slaying the Dragon: The History of Addiction Treatment and Recovery in America* by William White.

Throughout history, there has been a lot of uncertainty about how to handle addiction. Some see it as a spiritual problem, a moral problem, a mental health issue, or as a medical condition. As a result, there have been many varied approaches to addiction treatment. I will focus on the time of the late 1800's up to the present.

In the late 19th and early 20th Centuries, there was a proliferation of patent medicines. At that time, there were no controls or oversight over these medicines. Many of the medications that were offered to treat addiction contained opiates, cocaine, or, perhaps, alcohol. These "medications" were not examined by the government for safety or effectiveness, though their right for protection from being copied was protected by the Patent Office.

This changed as the dangers of the use of these medicines, particularly those with opiates, became evident. At that time the Pure Food and Drug Act and the Harrison Act were passed to try to protect the public.

One prime example of early medication assisted recovery is the Keeley Institute, founded in 1879, which offered the Keeley Cure, also known as the Gold Cure. They were well known at one time for their slogan, "Drunkenness is a disease and I can cure it."

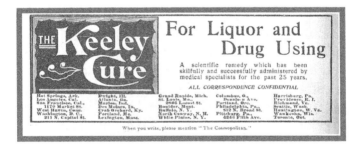

The Keeley Institute eventually had over 200 branches throughout the United States and Europe, and by 1900 the so-called Keeley Cure, injections of bichloride of gold, had been administered to more than 300,000 people.

The medical profession continued to criticize the method and many tried to identify the mysterious ingredients. Strychnine, alcohol, apomorphine, willow bark, and atropine were claimed to have been identified in the injections. The injections were dissolved in red, white and blue liquids and the amounts varied. In addition, patients would receive individually prescribed tonics every two hours throughout the day. Treatments lasted for a period of four weeks. Keeley claimed a rather hard-to-believe 95% success rate, bolstered by enthusiastic followers who formed Keeley Leagues, also known as Bi-Chloride of Gold Clubs.

By all reports, while the Gold Cure may not have really been that effective, the Keeley Institute did some things that were effective and would later be part of standard addiction treatment. They pioneered humane treatment of addicted people in a caring and supportive atmosphere; some say it was the first therapeutic community. It is interesting to note that the Institute had many doctors and nurses, but no counselors.

It was against this backdrop that Bill Wilson grew; as his alcoholism worsened, he had several hospitilizations at the Charles B. Townes Hospital for Drug and Alcohol Addictions in New York City, under the care of pioneering doctor William Silkworth. Despite Dr. Silkworth's efforts, he was unable to stop drinking. It was only when he met someone who found sobriety through the help of the Oxford Group, an Evangelical Christian organization, that Bill W., as he is commonly referred to in AA, found a way to stay sober.

People who followed the teachings of Alcoholics Anonymous found a success in sobriety that had been elusive to them. Since many had tried currently existing medications with no success, they felt that medication could not cure addiction, that only a spiritual experience could bring lasting sobriety.

They were right in believing that no medicine could cure addiction. Since addiction is a chronic disease, there is no cure; there have been, however, in the years since, some medications developed that can aid in the recovery process. We need to embrace these, not as a cure, but as part of the recovery process.

In the following pages I will give a brief overview of common medications used in modern addiction treatment. This information is in no way comprehensive or up-to-date. I highly suggest that you do an internet search to get more information on these medications.

Perhaps the oldest medication that is still in use to treat alcoholism is disulfiram, best known under the brand name Antabuse. The drug's action was discovered by accident in 1948 by researchers Erik Jacobsen, Jens Hald, and Kenneth Ferguson at the Danish drug company Medicinalco. The substance was intended to provide a remedy for parasitic infestations; however, workers testing the substance on themselves reported severe symptoms after alcohol consumption. This drug deters use of alcohol by providing negative effects with alcohol use. Some five to 10 minutes after alcohol intake, the person may experience the effects of a severe hangover for a period of 30 minutes up to several hours. Symptoms include flushing of the skin, an accelerated heart rate, shortness of breath, nausea and vomiting, visual disturbance, a throbbing headache, mental confusion, postural syncope, as well as circulatory collapse. The theory is that the negative effects will deter drinking. The effects of disulfiram may last up to two weeks after the last dose. A problem with this aversion method is that, unless medication compliance is monitored, it is very easy for a person to stop taking it, thus removing any deterence to using. There are still a number of people who use Antabuse as an aid for sobriety; it is also being investigated as a treatment for cocaine dependence, as it prevents the breakdown of dopamine.

Another medication with a fairly long history of use for treating addiction is methadone. Methadone is a synthetic opiate developed in Germany in 1937 to provide a reliable internal source of painkillers for their soldiers. Since it acts in the same manner as other opiates, it will help to prevent the withdrawal that occurs when a person who is dependent on opiates stops taking them.

The advantages to methadone include the fact that the effect has a long duration allowing a person to need only one dose per day. Since it can be taken orally in liquid form, there is no need to inject the drug, and it cannot be abused by crushing it and inhaling it. Since it is administered at a faciliy by health professionals, there is more quality and dose control.

Methadone maintenance began as a research project at The Rockefeller University in 1964, under the joint direction of Dr. Vincent P. Dole and Dr. Marie E. Nyswander. There was an increase in the use of heroin, and the relapse rates were high. It was decided that perhaps maintaining a person on a medically-supervised dose of methadone would be preferable to having people go through multiple treatment episodes with multiple relapses.

Methadone maintenance offers a harm-reduction approach to addiction. While the hoped-for, ultimate goal of the treatment is to be free from all substances, methadone treatment offers a safer alternative to using street drugs, Ideally, while on the medication, the person is also getting counseling to support their recovery. Since the medication is dispensed from specialized treatment facilities, counseling and other supports are offered in the program.

The newer maintenance drug used for treatment of opiate dependence is Suboxone. This is a form of buprenorphine, a semi-synthetic opiate. At low doses Buprenorphine produces sufficient agonist effect to enable opioid-addicted individuals to discontinue the misuse of opioids without experiencing withdrawal symptoms. The agonist effects of Buprenorphine increase linearly with increasing doses of the drug until it reaches a plateau and no longer continues to increase with further increases in dosage. This is called the "ceiling effect."

On the website of The National Alliance of Advocates for Buprenorphine Treatment, the following facts are offered:

Buprenorphine is different from other opioids in that it is a partial opioid agonist. This property of Buprenorphine may allow for;
- less euphoria and physical dependence
- lower potential for misuse
- a ceiling on opioid effects
- relatively mild withdrawal profile

At the appropriate dose buprenorphine treatment may:
- Suppress symptoms of opioid withdrawal
- Decrease cravings for opioids
- Reduce illicit opioid use
- Block the effects of other opioids
- Help patients stay in treatment

Suboxone combines buprenorphine with naloxone, which is often used to counteract the effects of opiate overdose. It was added to prevent crushing of Suboxone to inject it. Suboxone is now dispensed in a sub-lingual film.

The idea behind treatment with Suboxone was to get opiate treatment out of treatment centers that are often relegated to high-crime areas by zoning laws and community by-laws, and to bring it to the doctor's office. The difficulty this presents is a lack of easy access to the supportive systems such as counseling. On the positive side, however, people who are on Suboxone usually go to the doctor for a new prescription once a week at the start of treatment, quickly moving to a schedule of every three to four weeks if they are doing well. This makes it easier for people to maintain jobs and other life activities without needing to report daily for medication.

Another common drug used in addiction treatment is Naltrexone. In the original formulation, Naltrexone was used in treating opiate dependence as a way to block the euphoric effects of opiates. It differs from methadone and buprenorphine as it does not delay withdrawal. In fact, if Naltrexone is taken while opiates are in the system, a person will experience immediate withdrawal. As with Antabuse, compliance with taking the medication can be problem. To eliminate this problem, a long-acting, injectable form was created and is known as Vivitrol. Oddly, Vivitrol was first approved for the treatment of alcohol dependence. It seems to help reduce cravings for alcohol, and reduce heavy drinking. Vivitrol is now approved for both alcohol and opiate dependence treatment; though many who are opiate-addicted fear they cannot stay clean long enough to get opiates out of their system so they can begin treatment with Naltrxone.

The last medication I will discuss is acamprosate, sold under the brand name of Campral. In approving acamprosate, the FDA released this statement:

"While its mechanism of action is not fully understood, Campral is thought to act on the brain pathways related to alcohol abuse. Campral was demonstrated to be safe and effective by multiple placebo-controlled clinical studies involving alcohol-dependent patients who had already been withdrawn from alcohol, (i.e., detoxified). Campral proved superior to placebo in maintaining abstinence (keeping patients off alcohol consumption), as indicated by a greater percentage of acamprosate-treated subjects being assessed as continuously abstinent throughout treatment. Campral is not addicting and was generally well tolerated in clinical trials."

I have had several clients who were on Campral who reported good results from the medication. I have no idea if it was from the medication or if it was just the security of thinking they had extra help, but I do know that they stayed sober and engaged in treatment while on it.

As I have stated before, these medications do not cure addiction. They do, however, give the person a sense of well-being and physical support that allows them to engage in counseling to move toward lasting recovery. They are a useful tool and we need to support those who use these tools.

Chapter Three:
The Challenges of Medication Assisted Recovery

There are four major challenges that are faced when a clinician decides to work with clients in a MAR program. This chapter will outline the problems; subsequent chapters will offer tools and techniques that will help the clinician meet these challenges and can lead to successful client outcomes.

Counselor Attitudes and Beliefs

As mentioned earlier, traditionally, addiction treatment has been seen as a "drug-free" endeavor; indeed, many have highly questioned the validity of the medication-assisted recovery approach. There is very strong sentiment that those engaged in medication-assisted recovery programs are "not really in recovery." This attitude can be seen in professional treatment as well as in the self-help community.

One of the first things that we, as addiction treatment professionals, need to ask ourselves is whether we accept, or can accept, the premise of MAR. As newer medications are placed on the market, more people will opt for this approach. If a clinician is able to change his or her attitude to accept that medication can play a role in recovery, he or she is in a position to have a tremendous impact. If the clinican is not able to accept MAR then he or she is best to concentrate on working within the drug-free treatment community and to continue to have an impact there.

A frequent criticism of MAR is that the client is simply exchanging one drug for another. This is true of some medications that are being used at this time; some of the newer medications, however, especially those still in development and testing, are focused on balancing brain chemistry rather than preventing withdrawal and craving. In any case, the use of medication may be the best way to first bring a person into the recovery process.

Fear of withdrawal and its physical effects is a prime motivator for continued use of mood-altering substances even after the negative consequences of use outweigh any benefit that the drug provides. For many, the idea that a prescribed medication can eliminate the need to use illicit drugs is enough to bring them into treatment. If, in becoming involved in a MAR program, they are also exposed to the idea that continued recovery also requires work, skills, and support, the person is more likely to succeed in treatment. In order for clients to get this message there is a need for trained addiction counseling professionals who are willing and able to work with the client while they are engaged with their prescriber and are taking medication.

Another attitude or belief that the addiction professional must face is the idea that the ultimate goal of *all* clients should be total abstinence from all mood-altering substances. While that goal is ideal, the fact is that many of our clients, in both drug-free and MAR programs, do not come to us with a goal of total abstinence. If the client is faced with a forced choice to accept a goal of total abstinence or to leave treatment, many will choose to leave treatment, even if they have entered treatment under compulsion. The job of the addiction treatment professional is to meet the client wherever he or she is at and to hopefully help to move them toward a goal of total abstinence. This will be discussed more fully in a later chapter.

The most important thing is to recognize your attitudes and beliefs about medication-assisted recovery and to carefully decide if those attitudes and beliefs will allow you to work with clients in MAR. A good clinician may play a major role in the success of the client. If, however, the client feels they are being judged or manipulated into following the clinician's goals, the clinician could become a recovery barrier. There is nothing wrong with being opposed to MAR; but, if that is your attitude then you are best to not attempt this work. If you feel you can work with MAR clients then you have the possibility of reaching people who would not otherwise engage in the treatment process. This is, perhaps, the future of addiction treatment and we need to bring our skills and knowledge into this future.

Client Attitudes and Beliefs

One of the common charges leveled at medication-assisted recovery is that clients are looking for recovery without doing the work of recovery. There is some validity to this. Many clients in MAR programs feel that the medication will remove the cravings for use, thus eliminating the problem. Research, however, shows that in addiction, just as in the treatment of mood disorders, the combination of medication and therapy is the most efficient treatment. It is the role of the clinician to help the client recognize the difference between abstinence and recovery. The idea that simply abstaining from substance use equates to recovery is all too common. Often the client and his friends and family see abstinence as the goal. They fail to recognize that abstinence can be fleeting without a change in attitudes, beliefs, and behaviors.

Another common client belief is that one particular substance is the problem; if they can stop that substance, it is alright to continue use of other mood-altering substances. Thus, the client's goal may not agree with the goal of the treatment professionals. Other times the client's goal is not cessation of the drug of choice but simply "controlling" the use. This is less common in MAR, but does come up from time to time.

Frequently, clients involved in MAR have had previous experiences in addiction treatment programs and have made assumptions about the treatment they will receive from us. If they have ever taken part in a "drug-free" program while taking medication to assist recovery, they may very well expect to be judged and possibly rejected. They may feel that the clinician will want to exert his or her treatment plan rather than work with the client's wishes. They may feel that the clinician has nothing to offer if the clinician hasn't had the same experiences.

While this challenge is the client's, we as clinicians can help him or her meet this and find success in recovery.

Connecting With Prescibers

The growth of Medication Assisted Recovery has not only expanded treatment options; it has also moved treatment out of specialized addiction treatment facilities into the doctor's office. As a result, people who seek medication for recovery find themselves out of touch with those who can provide the cognitive and behavioral support they also need in order to be successful.

Many prescribers of medications for recovery have special, but limited, training in addiction issues in order to prescribe these medications. Some prescibers understand the need for a combination of medication and counseling, but others do not. It is the job of addiction counselors and other professionals to reach out to precribers and to form therapeutic alliances that help to assure that recovery becomes a reality.

It would be nice to believe that those physicians who choose to prescribe medication that assists in recovery would seek out area professionals, but that is not always the case. The addiction counselor needs to locate and reach out to prescribers and to form alliances with them. The pharmaceutical companies often provide web sites that list physicians who are trained to prescribe medications that treat addiction. I have gone to those lists and sent out information to the prescribers in my area outlining my services and requesting a chance to meet with them to discuss how we can work together to help their patients succeed in recovery. Some doctors like to have someone who will come to their office to allow their patients to make one trip for both services. Others prefer to have the patient go to a different facility. I have worked with some physicians who believe that all of their MAR clients should have counseling; others feel counseling is only needed if the patient continues to use alcohol or other drugs. I have found it is good to begin working with the doctor in the way they prefer; as I form an alliance with the prescriber I am better able to get them to reconsider our approach to best help the person in treatment.

Most addiction counseling professionals are not used to networking. For years, the clients have sought us out. If we want to continue to be an effective part of the recovery process, however, we need to become networkers.

Connecting With Clients

The increase in physician's office-based addiction treatment has brought about a major shift in the way people with addiction issues seek help. More and more we see people turning toward doctors for help with addiction rather than going to addiction treatment centers. Again, it is up to us as clinicians to make sure that clients know who we are, where we are, and to understand the power of the combination of medicine and counseling to bring about successful recovery.

Group or Individual?

Traditionally, a lot of addiction treatment is provided in the group setting. For treating people in MAR programs there are some things you must consider. If you choose to do group treatment you will need to have special groups for your medication assisted recovery clients. A mixed group would lead to many debates about the validity of MAR and could possibly prevent working on the real issues that both groups have in common. Also, clients in MAR do have specialized needs and issues that are unique to that modality. While group counseling allows people to share experiences and insights, individual counseling allows personalization of treatment.

In the long run, the best thing is to experiment and find what works best for you, the client, and the prescribing partner.

I offer a Medication Assisted Recovery group for those who seem to be coming merely to remain in compliance with their doctor's wishes. Those who indicate a deeper desire for change are moved into individual counseling. I use, among other techniques, Motivational Interviewing in the group to get clients further engaged in the recovery process.

The following chapters will explore ways that we can meet these challenges and will also present skills and techniques that are effective for medication-assisted recovery.

Chapter Four:
Client/Counselor Readiness for Treatment

Assessing Yourself

It is, perhaps, ironic that those of us in the counseling field, who encourage others in self-examination, are frequently reluctant to look at our own motivations and beliefs. If you are to consider counseling for MAR, however, it is important to be sure that you are fully able to commit yourself to the process.

One thing to examine is your path to working in the addiction field. Did you come to it through personal experience? The experience of others who are close to you? Did it seem like an area where you could contribute to society while utilizing your stregnths and skills?

You also need to look at your theory of addiction and recovery. Is it based on your own personal journey? Do you believe there is only one way to recover, or do you think that there is a need for individualized treatment that is geared toward the need of each client?

Do you have experience with people in MAR? Was it a positive or a negative experience? Did you see positives and negatives? What was your attitude toward the clients in that program?

Are you set in your ways or are you open to change and innovation? If you have reservations about MAR, are you able to set them aside to work with those who choose this route? These are important things to know.

The one thing that clients most expect from a counselor is acceptance; most are good at recognizing those who do not offer it freely. It has been shown that one of the most important predictors of success in treatment is a therapeutic alliance. The client needs to feel accepted and supported. If you feel there is any chance that you could not accept the client's choice to use medication as a part of their recovery program you owe it to yourself and the client to refer them to another therapist. If, on the other hand, you feel that medication assisted recovery can be a viable option, you are in a perfect position to help mold the addiction field as it changes and grows.

Assessing The Client

It is too easy for clinicians to get to a point where they begin to assume that the client's goals and the clinician's goals are the same; this is not always the case. In MAR it is especially important to determine the client's goals and desires. Some important questions to be asked are:

- What does the client hope to accomplish?
- What is the client's level of commitment to this goal?
- What is the client's motivation?
- What is the client willing to do to achieve his or her goal?

The answers to these questions are not so much to determine if the person is ready for treatment; these answers give the clinician a clear idea of how to structure the treatment. Once we know our ability and willingness to work within this framework and we understand where the client is in the process, we can begin to do the work we are trained to do.

Chapter Five:
Creating Connections

Marketing and networking have always been a part of the addiction treatment field; however it is more important than ever to make connections with a variety of people so that your program or practice continues to flourish. This is not only important for the sake of growing your business but also for the goal of reaching and helping those in need of our services.

Networking does not come naturally to many of us in this field; it may even sound somehow sleazy and demeaning. It seems rather intimidating to approach people to "sell yourself." One of the first things we need to do is to approach networking and marketing from a positive perspective.

The people that you will approach are those who generally share your concerns as well as your desire to help people change their lives. When you start to recognize that you are offering people something they really want and need, you feel less like a sales person and more like a healer who is sharing vital information with a colleague. That alone makes the process easier.

The next step is to determine who you need to contact. As I mentioned earlier, some of the medications used to treat addiction require the prescriber to get special certification before they can dispense the medication. The pharmaceutical companies offer a list of prescribers that is searchable by area. A search will identify doctors in your service area who are engaged in treating addiction. You can use that list to contact people who are probably quite anxious to find someone who can provide counseling to supplement their medical treatment of the problem. If clients come to your office for counseling and reveal that they are on a medication to treat addiction be sure to find out who is prescribing for them; some medications do not require special certification and the only way to find out who is prescribing these medications is through client self-report.

Some of the websites that list prescribers for medications also have a place where counselors can be listed. This allows both clients and prescribers to connect with addiction counselors who are comfortable working with those in MAR programs.

Keep in mind that these prescribers may have attempted to create partnerships with some local treatment programs and providers only to be told that the use of medication is not "true" recovery; this type of experience may have kept them from attempting to forge alliances with counselors. It is important to stress at the beginning of the encounter that you firmly believe that effective treatment can combine medication and therapy. This lets them know from the beginning that you are ready and willing to work with them and not against them.

I have found through experience that it is better to contact the prescriber's office by phone to request a time to meet with him or her. I tried mailing out information but did not get too much response; the personal approach seems the most effective.

Again, the pharmaceutical companies can be a good resource for networking as well. The sales representatives know the prescribers well and can help you to make contact with them. Some of the companies offer periodic trainings that bring together prescribers and clinicians. I highly suggest that you attend these if possible. I have had some salespersons act as brokers to connect me to prescribers who were looking for clinical partners.

There are a variety of ways that you can provide counseling for MAR clients. Some doctors request that you meet with their patients at their office so the two appointments can be coordinated. Others request specialized groups for MAR clients. Other prescribers leave the logistics to the clinician. The biggest challenge that I have faced as a private practitioner is insurance coverage. You may need to get creative in finding ways to provide service and still be paid.

You will need to remember to treat the prescriber as you would any good referral source. A Release of Information form should be signed and the prescriber should get regular reports of progress. It is good to check with each practitioner to help determine the type and amount of contact that is desired.

It is also important that we respect the doctor's approach and work within their framework. If we attempt to undermine the doctor's goals we not only lose the opportunity to be a part of the process, we also undermine the client's recovery.

The Medication Assisted Recovery model shifts the point of entry to treatment from specialized addiction treatment programs to the physician's office. Rather than see this as a threat, we need to see it and treat it as an opportunity to have more clients who need treatment as well as having strong partners in the recovery process.

Chapter Six:
Motivating Change

In an ideal world, everyone who comes to us for treatment would come with an understanding of their problem and a deep-felt determination to change. In fact, many, if not most, of the people I have seen for treatment come under some type of compulsion. The reason may be legal problems, or family pressure, some type of employment problems, or some other outside force that has the person presenting for treatment before they have determined the need for treatment. In MAR, it is quite common for the person to decide that they want to control addiction to one substance but not be committed to abstinence from all mood-altering drugs. While this does not mean that treatment is impossible, it does make it difficult.

If a client who enters our office does not feel he or she has a problem, it may be difficult to get them to fully engage; without engagement, change will not come about. Our first job, therefore, is to work with that person in a way that might help them come to their own decision to make changes in their life.

It is important for a clinician to recognize the process and stages of change. It is here that an understanding of the Stages of Change model and learning about the various Motivational Interviewing and Motivational Enhancement Therapy techniques becomes necessary.

In 1986, Prochaska and DiClemente developed the Stages of Change model. They identified five stages of change:

Pre-contemplation is the stage where the person is not yet convinced there is a problem or a need for change. A person who enters treatment at this phase is generally doing so under compulsion. As stated earlier, many of the clients I have seen over the years have entered treatment at this stage. The clinician's job at this point is to help the client recognize that they need to commit to recovery.

Contemplation is the stage where the person becomes aware that a problem exists and begins to think about doing something about it. Again, if a service recipient enters treatment at this stage, it is generally due to outside pressure. The clinician still needs to work with the client to engage them in treatment.

Preparation is a stage where a person is poised for action; they may even begin to make some attempt at change on their own. The person might even make the first move toward starting treatment, even though they are not totally convinced that they are ready to do this.

The *Action* stage is where the major change occurs. The person is committed to change and begins to do the work required for lasting recovery. This stage can take time, work, and energy. It is at this stage that the person has fully admitted the problem and makes a commitment to change. *Maintenance*, the fifth stage, is not a part of this discussion; it will be looked at in a later chapter.

The challenge of the clinician in most cases is to work with the client to help them move toward the Action stage. This can be accomplished in many ways; some ways, however, have been proven to more effective than others.

In the August, 2007 issue of *Counselor: The Magazine for Addiction Professionals,* William White and William Miller discuss the use of confrontation in addiction treatment. In the past, beginning around the 1920's and going on through the 1970's, confrontational therapy was widely used in addiction treatment. This approach was based on a theory that addicted people had defense mechanisms that were more highly developed than non-addicted people. The belief was that the job of the addiction professional was to "break 'em down to build 'em back up" (White and Miller, 2007). A series of clinical studies have since shown that harsh, confrontational approaches are not any more effective than other approaches. It is now believed that these approaches actually help to build and strengthen defense mechanisms, such as denial. Despite these findings, there are still a number of professionals in the addiction treatment field who rely on confrontational approaches.

I remember a time when I was asked to confront a client about a positive urine drug screen. My supervisor was trained during the days when harsh confrontational counseling was considered the best (perhaps only) way to help people with addiction; I am sure he felt I was too soft and could not be effective. I called the person into my office and stated that the recent screen was positive. She immediately denied using. I explained that I was not looking to get her into trouble and was not planning to discharge her from treatment; I merely wanted to know how she was doing so I could better help her. She still denied drug use. I then calmly pointed out that she had given the sample, and had verified that the sample was hers. I asked her, if she hadn't used drugs, how she felt the drugs had gotten into the sample. She hesitated for a moment, and then finally admitted that she had used cocaine due to having a headache. After pointing out to her that most people would have used aspirin, I then helped her to plan how she could prevent this from happening again. As it turned out, that was her last drug use during treatment; to my knowledge, she is still maintaining her recovery several years later.

I had, in fact, confronted this client. I just did not use the usual confrontation style that has been popular in addiction treatment. What I did was more along the lines of Motivational Interviewing. This is an approach to addiction treatment that is gaining popularity; one reason for this increased popularity is that it has been proven effective in many clinical trials.

Motivational Interviewing (MI), developed by Stephen Rollnick and William R. Miller, is a client-centered, directive method for enhancing intrinsic motivation to change by exploring and resolving ambivalence. The following information, from the official Motivational Interviewing website, offers an interesting look at this approach.

"We believe it is vital to distinguish between the *spirit* of motivational interviewing and *techniques* that we have recommended to manifest that spirit. Clinicians and trainers who become too focused on matters of technique can lose sight of the spirit and style that are central to the approach. There are as many variations in technique as there are clinical encounters. The spirit of the method, however, is more enduring and can be characterized in a few key points. *Motivation to change is elicited from the client, and not imposed from without.* Other motivational approaches have emphasized coercion, persuasion, constructive confrontation, and the use of external contingencies (e.g., the threatened loss of job or family). Such strategies may have their place in evoking change, but they are quite different in spirit from motivational interviewing which relies upon identifying and mobilizing the client's intrinsic values and goals to stimulate behavior change."

1. *It is the client's task, not the counselor's, to articulate and resolve his or her ambivalence.* Ambivalence takes the form of a conflict between two courses of action (e.g., indulgence versus restraint), each of which has perceived benefits and costs associated with it. Many clients have never had the opportunity of expressing the often confusing, contradictory and uniquely personal elements of this conflict, for example, "If I stop smoking I will feel better about myself, but I may also put on weight, which will make me feel unhappy and unattractive." The counselor's task is to facilitate expression of both sides of the ambivalence impasse, and guide the client toward an acceptable resolution that triggers change.

2. *Direct persuasion is not an effective method for resolving ambivalence.* It is tempting to try to be "helpful" by persuading the client of the urgency of the

problem and about the benefits of change. It is fairly clear, however, that these tactics generally increase client resistance and diminish the probability of change (Miller, Benefield and Tonigan, 1993, Miller and Rollnick, 1991).

3. *The counseling style is generally a quiet and eliciting one.* Direct persuasion, aggressive confrontation, and argumenttation are the conceptual opposite of motivational interviewing and are explicitly proscribed in this approach. To a counselor accustomed to confronting and giving advice, motivational interviewing can appear to be a hopelessly slow and passive process. The proof is in the outcome. More aggressive strategies, sometimes guided by a desire to "confront client denial," easily slip into pushing clients to make changes for which they are not ready.

4. *The counselor is directive in helping the client to examine and resolve ambivalence.* Motivational interviewing involves no training of clients in behavioral coping skills, although the two approaches not incompatible. The operational assumption in motivational

interviewing is that ambivalence or lack of resolve is the principal obstacle to be overcome in triggering change. Once that has been accomplished, there may or may not be a need for further intervention such as skill training. The specific strategies of motivational interviewing are designed to elicit, clarify, and resolve ambivalence in a client-centered and respectful counseling atmosphere.

5. *Readiness to change is not a client trait, but a fluctuating product of interpersonal interaction.* The therapist is therefore highly attentive and responsive to the client's motivational signs. Resistance and "denial" are seen not as client traits, but as feedback regarding therapist behavior. Client resistance is often a signal that the counselor is assuming greater readiness to change than is the case, and it is a cue that the therapist needs to modify motivational strategies.

6. *The therapeutic relationship is more like a partnership or companionship than expert/recipient roles.* The therapist respects the client's autonomy and freedom of choice (and consequences) regarding his or her own behavior.

Viewed in this way, it is inappropriate to think of motivational interviewing as a technique or set of techniques that are applied to or (worse) "used on" people. Rather, it is an interpersonal style, not at all restricted to formal counseling settings. It is a subtle balance of directive and client-centered components shaped by a guiding philosophy and understanding of what triggers change. If it becomes a trick or a manipulative technique, its essence has been lost (Miller, 1994).

With that having been said, there are techniques that are commonly used in Motivational Interviewing. I will give a brief overview of these here; I highly recommend that you visit the official Motivational Interviewing website to obtain detailed information. The web address is www.motivationalinterview.org.

The basic techniques of MI are found in the acronym *OARS:* **O**pen-ended questions, **A**ffirmations, **R**eflective listening, and **S**ummaries. I will briefly look at each of these techniques.

Open-ended questions are questions that cannot be answered by *yes* or *no*. A closed question allows a response but does not encourage further communication or exploration. "What brings you here today?" is a question that will result in a far different answer than asking, "Did you come because you think you have a problem?" Open-ended questions not only allow, but encourage openness and sharing.

Affirmations can help a client to feel fully accepted, capable to make change, and helps to build a sense of hope. Affirmations, however, must appear sincere. These affirmations are not simply general, positive statements; they are personal observations of the client's positive qualities and accomplishments.

Reflective listening is the key to this work. This is so important, that the following information is directly from the MI website as I couldn't word it better:

"The best motivational advice we can give you is to listen carefully to your clients. They will tell you what has worked and what hasn't. What moved them forward and shifted them backward. Whenever you are in doubt about what to do, listen. But remember this is a directive approach. Unlike Rogerian therapists, you will actively guide the client towards certain materials. You will focus on their change talk and provide less attention to non-change talk. For example, 'You are not quite sure you are ready to make a change, but you are quite aware that your drug use has caused concerns in your relationships, affected your work and that your doctor is worried about your health.'

You will also want to vary your level of reflection. Keeping reflections at the surface level may lead to that feeling that the interaction is moving in circles. Reflections of affect, especially those that are unstated but likely, can be powerful motivators. For example, 'Your children aren't living with you anymore; that seems painful for you.' If you are right, the emotional intensity of the session deepens. If you are wrong or the client is unready to deal with this material, the client corrects you and the conversation moves forward.

The goal in MI is to create forward momentum and to then harness that momentum to create change. Reflective listening keeps that momentum moving forward. This is why the developers of MI recommend a ratio of three reflections for every question asked. Questions tend to cause a shift in momentum and can stop it entirely. Although there are times you will want to create a shift or stop momentum, most times you will want to keep it flowing."

Summaries are really another form of reflective listening. They help to recap what has been said and what insights have been gained. MI suggests doing them frequently so the amount of information to be summarized is not too overwhelming. Effective use of summaries allows important information to be repeated; this repetition helps people to retain the information.

The purpose of Motivational Interviewing is to help the client to commit to change. As discussed earlier in the chapter, while total abstinence is perhaps the best and ultimate goal, it may be necessary to move a client toward a goal of abstinence in stages. I have found that those clients who are mandated to treatment are especially reluctant to commit to a lifetime of abstinence. I have seen many people rebel against enforced abstinence to the point that they decide they would rather leave treatment and face the consequences than to stay in treatment being told what is right for them.

I have found it better to set short-term goals for people in these situations. I have told mandated clients, "The court says you have to complete this program in order to keep your license and stay out of jail. I can't tell you what to do with your life, but, you will come out for the better if you can stay away from alcohol and drugs for the next six months." I have had many people begin with that six-month commitment who have moved to a commitment for total abstinence before their treatment was complete.

When a client states he or she doesn't see the need to stay clean and sober, I try to help them to explore the ambivalence. I might say, "It sounds like you would rather face jail time or losing your license than to be told what to do. This must be important to you" That statement can sometimes help a person to see flaws in their thinking.

Making a commitment to a path of recovery may take time. The important thing is, however, that this commitment must come from the client. Our job is to help move the client toward that commitment.

As I stated earlier, our clients in MAR may have different goals than we are used to as we begin to work together. If we meet them where they are at we are in a good position, as time goes on, to keep them re-evaluating their goals and perhaps making deeper commitment to complete recovery.

Chapter Seven:
Self Awareness and Connection

As people become more deeply involved in the process of addiction, they lose connection with the basic sense of self. While they may believe that they have "self-control," it is actually the desire or need for the substance that is controlling them. In addiction, the person is *re*acting rather than acting. As a person begins the process of recovery, he or she needs to restore and strengthen the sense of self.

The topic of "self" is one of the basics of psychology. There are a variety of personality development theories; each theory of development leads to a theory of restoring a "disturbed" person to a healthy balance. Some theories are based on "nature;" they state that a person's personality is based on genetic influences. Other theories are "nurture" based, stating that environmental influences form the personality or self. There are some theories that suggest that personality is based on a third element, which is frequently defined as the "soul." Combining elements of these three approaches leads to what I feel is a workable theory of self as it applies to the process of addiction and recovery.

Perhaps the first task is to define the term, "self." In *Psychology of Adjustment* (Sawrey and Telford, 1971), the self is defined as having three aspects: the physical self, the social self, and the self-concept. The physical self is our first discovery as infants. It expands as our physical awareness of our bodies continues to evolve. As we become more aware of our environment, we develop the social self, which is the way we respond to others in our surroundings. "The child very early in life accepts as valid other people's judgments of him and his characteristics" (Sawrey and Telford,1971). These judgments help to build the self-concept. Unfortunately, for a number of people, these judgments are not always valid. Frequently, they are the sole basis of the self-concept.

This definition of self is, perhaps, compatible with many personality theories. It includes both nature and nurture. There is, however, an element that is missing. Sawrey and Telford state, "The self-concept is more important than the 'real self' in determining behavior" (Sawrey and Telford, 1971). What they fail to do, however, is to define the "real self."

The real self, which I prefer to call the true self, is indeed, much harder to define. In *The Thirst for Wholeness: Attachment, Addiction, and the Spiritual Path*, Christina Grof (1993) calls it the Deeper Self, which is connected with a divine force. John Firman and Ann Gila, in *The Primal Wound: A Transpersonal View of Trauma, Addiction and Growth* (1997), speak of the true self and the Transpersonal Self, which is also considered to be a part of a greater force. Karen Walant speaks of the Alienated Self in her book, *Creating the Capacity for Attachment: Treating*

Addictions and the Alienated Self (1995). It is difficult, in fact, to find a definition for the true self that does not include some sort of spiritual aspect.

Spirituality is important to many people, and it can be a useful tool in recovery. It is possible, however, to view the true self and to recover from addiction without spirituality. I have developed what I feel is a rational, cognitive definition of true self.

The true self is the basis of our personality before we are influenced by the beliefs, both rational and irrational, that help make up the social self; it should be a major part of our self-concept. The true self is inherent in all people; there are aspects of it that do not rely on nature or nurture.

I would, then, state that there are four aspects of self: the physical self, the social self, the self-concept, and the true self. The process of recovery involves restoring connection to the true self and rebuilding the self-concept in a manner that more accurately reflects the true self.

A common theme in the literature on addiction and self is the addict's sense of emptiness or being alone. Craig Nakken, in *The Addictive Personality: Understanding Compulsion in Our Lives* (1988) states that, "no matter what the addiction is, every addict engages in a relationship with an object or event in order to produce a desired mood change." The mood change is needed to fill a sense of emptiness. While there are a number of ways of defining that sense of emptiness, I see it as the need for the true self.

There has also been a tendency in addiction treatment to undervalue the need for self-awareness and self-sufficiency. The general belief is that the self is what led to the addiction, and something beside the self is needed to overcome the addiction. The addict is seen as being self-centered, which contributes to the addiction. It is my view that disconnection from the true self is what keeps the addiction active and that true self-awareness will aid recovery. Nakken (1998) makes a very compelling argument for this view in the following statement:

> "Some people say that addicts are self-centered. I strongly disagree. Instead, addicts are Addict-centered at a cost to the Self. The process of recovery from the illness of addiction is found in Self-renewal. For us to recover, there has to be a rededication or dedication to Self. In other words, the Self must become important again" (Nakken, 1998).

The "Self" that Nakken refers to is what I call the true self, which needs to become a major influence on the self-concept.

There is a strong belief that there is a genetic predisposition to alcohol and drug addiction. It is also obvious that the physical effects of alcohol and other drugs affect the physical self; this, in turn, affects the self-concept. Once the presence or absence of a substance defines the physical self and the self-concept adapts to that definition, the person is separated to a degree from the true self.

As the social self develops, the person is exposed to various messages that also help to build the self-concept. Some of these messages are accurate gauges of the person and their interactions with others. There are messages, however, that reflect the self-concept of others; these messages may not accurately apply to the developing person. If that person should incorporate them into the developing self-concept, the result is a disconnection between the true self and the self-concept.

While the self-concept begins its formation early in life, it is not static. The self-concept continues to change and grow as a person experiences life. This self-concept may play a role in the person's addiction; at the same time, the addiction also plays a role in the self-concept.

If a person grows up in an addicted family, the self-concept of that person can be built on inaccurate messages. Some may feel as though they are the cause of problems in the family. Others may believe that life is unpredictable and that there is no prevailing sense of order. Some may come to believe that mood-altering substances are a necessary coping strategy for life. There are countless irrational messages that can be incorporated into the self-concept when a person grows up in an addicted household. A person can incorporate similar messages even if they do not grow up in an addicted environment, but the chances of these influences are increased by their presence in an addicted family.

Once a person begins the process of addiction the outside influences on the self-concept become powerful enough to cause a further disconnection from the true self. As the need for the substance becomes more powerful, the physical self more heavily influences the self-concept. As a person becomes more physically dependent on a substance, interactions with others begin to change. This affects the self-concept.

In addiction, a person may begin to distrust feedback from other people as these people are expressing concern about the extent of the effects of the substance on the person and their relationships. At the same time, guilt and shame may also influence the self-concept. The addicted person may have difficulty accepting that their behavior is a result of the substance and may begin to view him or her self as "bad." As a result, their self-concept becomes based on the idea that they are in some way flawed.

As addiction progresses, the person may become involved in behaviors that are far removed from the true self. They are caught within a self-concept that is shaped and defined by drug use. They must use the drug in order to meet the expectations of that addicted self-concept.

As we consider recovery from addiction, it is important to realize that abstinence from alcohol and drug use is only the start of a long and difficult process. Recovery from addiction must include recovery of the true self and incorporation of the true self into the self-concept. This is neither as easy nor as difficult as it may sound. There are a number of things that can be done to help restore connection with the true self; these things take time, effort, and patience, but they are effective.

It is important to identify what comprises the true self. This is a process of self-examination. I have found several questions are helpful in this process. First, a person needs to examine beliefs. What do I believe about myself? What do I believe about others? What do I believe about the world around me?

Once these beliefs are known, it may be necessary to examine them to determine if they are rational or irrational. Irrational beliefs lead to a disconnection from the true self. These can be disputed using the REBT techniques outlined in the next chapter. Rational beliefs can be used to strengthen the connection with the true self.

Other questions also can be used to redefine and rebuild the true self. What is important to me? What moral or ethical guidelines do I feel that I must follow? What must I have to feel fulfilled and at peace? What do I want from life for myself and for others? These questions require careful thought. It is important to differentiate between what the individual really wants and needs and what they have been made to feel they want and need.

Another way to reconnect with the true self is to evaluate strengths and weaknesses. During active addiction a person tends to lose track of both of these. They feel too weak to acknowledge strengths and too strong to admit to any weakness. Making a list of strengths and weaknesses gives a person a clearer view of the true self, for these are components of the true self. When a person can acknowledge both strengths and weaknesses, they also achieve a balanced sense of self.

Meditation is also an effective method of connecting with the true self. This is not necessarily a "spiritual" practice; meditation is quieting the mind, getting beyond the social self, to hear the voice of the true self. There is no special way to meditate to connect with the true self, no mantras or special positions. A person simply needs to find a quiet space, a comfortable position, and to allow everyday thoughts and concerns to be forgotten. In the quiet, a person's "inner voice" becomes clearer. During this process a person may become more aware of inner messages; these can then be evaluated to determine if they are affirming or destructive messages.

Guided visualization can also be effective in connecting with the true self. While it is similar to meditation, it is also a form of self-hypnosis. Again, the focus is on relaxation and clearing the mind of everyday thoughts and concerns. In guided visualizations, however, spoken suggestions are given to help guide the person's thinking in a way to promote self-awareness. In a visualization to connect with the true self, the suggestions would probably include walking a path, going deeper into a place such as a forest. The person would be instructed to continue relaxing as they travel the path. The person might be instructed to take note of any obstacles found on the path, but to move past the obstacles. The person would be led to a clearing where they will take time to notice the surroundings, thoughts, and feelings. The person would then be brought back along the path to their starting point. These visualizations can be relaxing and informative. Recorded guided visualizations are available, or a person may record his or her own visualization. There is a sample visualization in the appendix of this book.

These approaches to restoring connection with the true self are, at first, uncomfortable for people in recovery. I have had many clients voice reluctance at spending time reflecting on the questions of beliefs, values and needs. Often, they will give quick, short, and superficial answers to those questions. I have had people tell me later that the questions prompted them to really reflect and that they have been surprised at what they discovered.

Many of them also note that their actions have been very far removed from their beliefs and values. This leads them to begin building a new self-concept that is more closely aligned to the true self.

In the Twelve-Step approach, there is an emphasis on finding a "Higher Power," which is generally considered to be a supernatural power known as God. This works for many people, but does not work for everyone. For those who have trouble with the concept of God, I feel that this higher power can be the true self. When a person in recovery finds the true self, they have found a power that is greater than the self-concept that was created through, and kept alive through, their addiction. If the person does indeed have a spiritual basis the need for self-awareness and connection is still an important part of the recovery process.

Chapter Eight:
Cognitive/Behavioral Techniques in MAR

This chapter will examine the history of Rational Emotive Behavior Therapy (REBT) as developed by Albert Ellis. It will also explore how Ellis has applied it to addiction treatment and how Jack Trimpey, founder of Rational Recovery, expanded this application. I will briefly comment on the struggle between Rational Recovery and Alcoholics Anonymous. Finally, I will discuss how these techniques are useful for treating people in Medication Assisted Recovery programs.

Albert Ellis, founder of REBT, was trained in psychoanalysis. Over time, Ellis began to doubt the effectiveness of psychoanalysis, with its emphasis on uncovering past traumas. Ellis came to believe that discovering the faulty beliefs that led to irrational behaviors could treat the problems that his patients presented. In 1955, Ellis first developed Rational Emotive Therapy (RET). Ellis changed this to Rational Emotive Behavior Therapy (REBT) around 1995. For the sake of clarity, and to acknowledge Ellis' continued work, I will refer to it as REBT. This approach was first presented in the 1957 book, *How to Live with a Neurotic*. The definitive book on the subject was *A Guide to Rational Living*, written by Ellis and Robert Harper, first published in 1961.

Ellis believes that the basis of most emotional disturbance is the presence of irrational beliefs. His philosophy is often briefly stated as "you feel what you feel because you think what you think." In other words, people do not respond to specific events; they react to what they *believe* about the event. If the person has an irrational belief, the event will trigger an irrational response. REBT offers the following formula to demonstrate the process:

A ←→ B ←→ C
(activating event) (belief) (emotional / behavioral consequence)

To help clarify this approach, I will present a "real life" example of this theory. John is currently in treatment for cocaine dependence. His wife, Mary, tells him, "I have been hurt by your actions while you were using." John pulls away from his wife and begins to curse and throw things. John is not reacting to what Mary said. If he were, he would not have such an extreme reaction. John is reacting to irrational beliefs that he holds. Perhaps he believes that he is unlovable unless he is perfect. It may be that he believes that any negative feedback is total rejection. Whatever the belief may be, the consequence is in reaction to the belief, not the event.

REBT offers a way to deal with these messages. First, a person needs to identify the irrational messages that affect them. To do this, the person would review situations that resulted in irrational responses to events. They would then try to determine the belief that led to the response. After the beliefs are identified, they would use a disputing intervention to arrive at a rational effect and a new feeling. Here is an expansion of the earlier diagram, showing the REBT process:

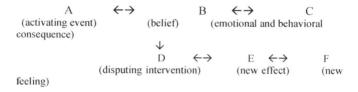

In this diagram, "D" is the disputing intervention; a three-step process designed to challenge the irrational beliefs. After first detecting the irrational belief, the person debates these beliefs by learning how to logically question them and effectively stop believing them. The third step is to discriminate rational beliefs from irrational beliefs. This disputing technique leads to "E," an effective, rational philosophy. This philosophy helps create "F," a new set of feelings.

To return to the earlier example, John would examine his irrational response to Mary's statement. He may discover that he has the irrational belief that any negative feedback is total rejection. He disputes this by telling himself that no one is perfect, and Mary has the right to feel as she does. He tells himself that he is still acceptable even though he may have faults. As a result, he is better able to respond to Mary and others who give him constructive criticism. This leads to a new feeling that is based on rational thought.

REBT suggests that pronounced feelings of failure, beliefs in worthlessness, unthinking acceptances of other's condemnation, and self-damning tendencies are not justified, "not because they emerge as absolutely wrong or wicked, or because they contradict the laws of God or the universe. But simply because, on good pragmatic grounds, they almost always prove self-defeating and needlessly prevent us from getting many of the things that we desire" (Ellis & Harper, 1975).

There are five core irrational beliefs that people are likely to hold. The first one is identified by Ellis as "Musturbation," also known as shoulding or demandingness. An example of this is the belief, "I have to (should, must, ought to, deserve to) do well and be approved by people I like or else I am an inadequate, worthless person!" Almost any beliefs with words like must, should, ought, or deserve are likely to be irrational. Awfulizing beliefs are identified in this sentence, "It's awful, terrible, horrible, catastrophic when I don't perform well (as I must), when you don't give me what I need (as you should), and when conditions frustrate me (as they must not)!" Low Frustration Tolerance is identified in statements such as, "I can't stand (bear, tolerate) it when I don't get what I need (as I must) or when I do get what I don't want (and must not get)." Rating and blaming beliefs can be, "I am a worthless and damnable person for behaving poorly (as I must not behave)!" Finally, overgeneralizing, an always or never attitude, can be seen in the belief, "When I do poorly (as I must not) or things are bad (as they must not be), that proves I'll never be happy, succeed, or get what I want" (Ellis & Velton, 1992).

Some people may feel these statements are so extreme that no one could possibly hold them as beliefs. In my experience, they are really quite common, especially among people with substance addiction problems. The use of REBT techniques to dispute these messages can provide a person with a way to eliminate the message as well as the consequence of the belief.

Ellis presents REBT as an effective tool for treating chemical dependency. He co-authored two books that explore the use of REBT for addictions. *When AA Doesn't Work for You: Rational Steps for Quitting Alcohol*, written with Emmett Velton, is written for the layperson, while *Rational Emotive Therapy with Alcoholics and Substance Abusers*, written with John McInerney, Raymond DiGiuseppe, and Raymond Yeager is a professional's guide. In *When AA Doesn't Work for You: Rational Steps for Quitting Alcohol*, the authors present REBT's three insights. These are:

> *Insight One*: Your current feelings and actions have causes. The most important causes of your addictions are your thoughts, attitudes, images, memories, and other cognitions. This is what REBT calls B, your belief system, especially your stinking thinking or irrational beliefs.

Insight Two: Wherever your belief systems originated (parents, family, society, traumas, biology, self-inventions), you carry them on now and actively believe and follow them. You steadily reindoctrinate yourself in them today and sometimes actively fight off other's attempts to get you to change them.

Insight Three: You require hard, persistent work to change your beliefs, actions, and feelings, to practice new ones, and to avoid returning to old ones. Further, your human condition tends to give new problems and stresses. So insight is not the main watchword. Eternal vigilance plus much work and practice is (Ellis & Velton, 1992).

This approach stands somewhat in opposition to a strict disease model of addiction, but is not totally inconsistent with the disease model presented in the first chapter. It acknowledges that biology may play a role in addiction as it could affect irrational beliefs. It also acknowledges the role that cognition plays in recovery. This approach differs from AA as it suggests that people have the power to change their beliefs; this is in contrast to the AA statement that a person is powerless over their addiction.

In *Rational Emotive Therapy with Alcoholics and Substance Abusers*, Ellis offers more specific information on ways that beliefs can affect recovery and ways to deal with those beliefs. One attitude or belief that is common is that abstinence from mood-altering substances is a curse. A person with that belief will find that recovery is a burden and is likely to return to using. That person can use the techniques of REBT to change the belief to one of recovery as an opportunity to improve the quality of life.

Another attitudinal barrier is self-pity. If a person feels sorry for himself or herself because other people can use substances "responsibly" while they cannot, they may decide to go back to substance use no matter the consequence. People with this attitude need to tell themselves that other people are able to do a lot of things that they cannot do; what matters is what they *can* do, which includes living a clean and sober life.

Some people will think, "Drinking and drugging is not a problem for me; it is other people who have a problem with the way I drink and use." The rational belief for disputing that is, "If my drinking or using is a problem for others, it soon will be for me if it is not already a problem."

Another common attitude is that sobriety will be too hard, and the person might lose friends, be bored or uncomfortable. To combat that attitude, people should tell themselves that, while it may take some time and effort, they may lose much more if they continue to use.

Feeling as though they cannot stand to not have another drink or drug is another common attitude for people in recovery. They need to admit that abstinence is difficult, but they have endured other difficulties in the past. They should also remember that, while they may *want* to have another drink or drug, they do not *need* to have it (Ellis, et. al., 1988).

Another contribution to cognitive treatment of addiction is the work of Jack Trimpey, founder of Rational Recovery. Mr. Trimpey is a person who has dealt with his own alcohol problem; like many, he first went to AA to try to find help. Trimpey found the religious aspects of AA, and the "our way or the highway" attitude of many within the group, to be too uncomfortable. As a result, he decided to develop another approach to treating addiction. As a practicing social worker, Trimpey was familiar with Ellis and the REBT process. Trimpey used this as a basis for his Rational Recovery program.

Trimpey has added important techniques to cognitive/behavioral addiction treatment of addiction. These techniques, however, are protected by proprietary trademark, so I will not elaborate on them. He presents his views in two books, *The Small Book*, and *Rational Recovery: The New Cure for Substance Addiction*. These techniques are extremely useful and, on the surface, appear to be acceptable to anyone in recovery. Yet, there is great enmity and argument between Rational Recovery (RR) and Alcoholics

Anonymous (AA). I feel that the reasons for this need to be.

Prior to the founding of AA, treatment of alcoholism was not highly effective. AA appeared to work for many people. As AA became widely publicized, people in the treatment community began to see AA as "the answer"- the only way that people could recover from alcohol addiction. These same principles were then applied to drug users through Narcotics Anonymous.

The problem with viewing any form of addiction treatment as the only form of treatment is that it does not take into account the diversity of human beings. Just as some people are helped by a medication that causes an allergic reaction in others, not all people will respond to a specific mode of treatment. AA may work well for some; for others the approach may cause extreme adverse reactions.

The creation of RR would seem to solve a problem, offering people in treatment, and treatment providers, a choice of treatment approaches. Unfortunately, this is not what happened. Part of the problem undoubtedly lies in the fact that there are those who staunchly present AA as the only effective treatment approach for addiction, and who accuse anyone presenting a differing view of practicing bad medicine and jeopardizing the lives of people with addiction problems.

Another part of the problem is the manner in which Trimpey presented his Rational Recovery approach. For example, the "bible" of AA is the book, *Alcoholics Anonymous*, which is commonly known as "the Big Book." The title of Trimpey's first book, *The Small Book*, was an obvious poke at AA. The book seems to spend as much time talking about what is wrong with AA as it does explaining RR. Three of the thirteen chapters of the book contain the words "take sides." It is not surprising that RR offended people in AA.

I believe that there is a need for multiple treatment approaches to treat the diverse population of people with addiction. Rather than present any program as "the" program, we need to have a variety of options to choose from. In addition, treatment providers and clients should feel free to blend treatment approaches in order to best meet the needs of each individual. As Dianne Doyle Pita states in her book, *Addictions Counseling*, "There are enough addicted people to go around. No one needs to corner the market" (Pita, 1998).

Cognitive/Behavioral Therapy is considered an evidence-based treatment approach; it has become an integral part of many treatment programs. It works especially well in the MAR treatment plan as well as in drug-free treatment.

Irrational messages play a major role in the development and continuation of addictive disease. MAR counselors need to stress the need to become aware of these irrational messages and encourages the use of REBT to dispute those messages.

I use these techniques with the clients I see. It is not at all unusual to have a client tell me that "I wanted to use," or "I needed the drug." I have them look at the statement and to learn to change the "I wanted/needed" to "It wanted/needed." I have had several clients report that this technique alone has increased their ability to resist drug use. Several other clients have reported discovering irrational beliefs that have led them to drug use. Most clients need to be reminded that overcoming irrational beliefs is a process; many expect the messages to disappear once they have been identified and wonder what they have done wrong because the belief returns.

REBT is a great, short-term approach for treating addiction and is, therefore, especially good for those in medication assisted recovery programs. The person's engagement with us may have a limited period of time, especially if insurance companies are involved. REBT allows us to teach skills in a short period of time that the person can practice over the course of their lives. It is not a replacement for long-term recovery support, but it does have a life beyond the counseling relationship. The use of REBT is as consistent with twelve-step based treatment and can only improve the effectiveness of addiction treatment.

Chapter Nine:
Communication Skills For Recovery

Surprisingly, very little is said about the importance of communication in the process of recovery. A literature search using the key words "addiction" and "communication" did not offer a single match. I find this interesting, as I believe communication plays a vital role in the recovery process.

In my mind, communication is a vital part of many of the recovery process. In order to take responsibility for past actions a person must be able to express their regret in a manner that allows the person to whom it is addressed to comprehend and respond appropriately. Communication is also important in identifying and expressing feelings. Communication is also needed to restore connection with significant people and to make connection with others who will support recovery.

Communication also is needed to let the addiction professionals know the level of the client's compliance with treatment and the areas that they need to work on. If the person cannot communicate these needs, the doctors and counselors cannot be fully effective.

This idea is fully supported by the work of Carl Rogers. He states that a "neurotic" person is in trouble first because he or she cannot communicate within his or her self; and, as long as this is true, there are distortions in the way the person communicates with others. He further states that the task of counseling is to first improve the inner communication and then to improve communication with others (Rogers, 1961). In SCARF, the inner communication is learned as a person restores the true self. The next task is to improve communication with others.

In the following pages I will present some basics of communication theory that help to set a foundation for rules of communication. I will briefly discuss the effect of rational and irrational beliefs on communication. Finally, I will present a number of communication skills that will aid the recovery process.

At the heart of communication theory is the concept of the sender and the receiver. Take, for example, a radio station and your car radio. The station sends out the message, but there is no guarantee that you will receive that message. If you are not in the car, you will not receive it. If the radio is off, you will not receive it. If you are tuned to a different station, you will not receive it. If you drive out of range of the station, you will not receive it. The same holds true for interpersonal communication.

There are many things that can prevent a message from being received in interpersonal communication. I will look at these in more detail later, but some common problems are differences of interpretation, irrational beliefs, and inattentive listening.

In *Bridges Not Walls: A Book about Interpersonal Communication*, John Stewart presents five basic facts about communication. They are:

1. No one person can completely control a communication event, and no single person or action causes – or can be blamed for – a communication outcome.

2. Culture figures prominently in the communication process. Ethnicity, gender, age, social class, sexual orientation, and other cultural features always affect communication and are affected by it.

3. Some of the most important meanings people collaboratively construct are identities; all communication involves negotiating identities or selves.

4. The most influential communication events are conversations.

5. The most useful single communication skill is "nexting," which is asking yourself, "What can I help to happen next, or how?" (Stewart, 1999)

Each of these facts holds an important message about communication. The first one makes the point that communication is something that involves two or more people; each plays a role in the process. As a result, all parties have responsibility for the successful, or unsuccessful, outcome of the communication event. This requires that all parties make an effort to keep the process moving efficiently.

I feel that the most important point made by Stewart in the above is the second, that of the effect of culture on communication. I remember one of my adolescent clients who commented on the Birkenstock shoes I was wearing. The comment was, "Those are really fat shoes." I began to respond that, while the toe was wider than normal, they weren't really fat. The client laughed at this point, and explained that they were "phat," meaning, to my generation, cool. This is an example of the effect of culture on communication.

This applies as well to differences in socialization. While men and women may not be from different planets, their social training is usually different. Women may be raised to value specific traits, such as openness and vulnerability; men are often taught that these traits are signs of weakness. Racial, economic, and social differences can also result in differing values and understandings. When communication seems blocked, it may be the result of such differences.

The third fact simply points out that identity issues are always involved in communication. A person's self-image has an affect on the way they listen and respond in a communication event. This can especially come into play where irrational messages affect a person's self-image.

The fourth fact points out that conversation, our most ordinary form of communication, is also the most important. This is one reason for learning communication skills. The fifth fact points out that the most important communication skill is to keep the communication flowing.

Communication is an important part of any relationship. Effective communication requires listening skills as well as speaking skills. Before we can listen to others, however, we must be able to listen to ourselves. Many people feel that self-awareness is a selfish thing. In reality, it is vital to any type of interaction in life. Our relationship to other people, to nature, and to society is affected by our ability to know and to accept ourselves.

I explored the effects of subconscious, irrational messages in the examination of the use of cognitive/behavioral techniques in MAR. These messages can be a major hindrance to any type of communication. That chapter demonstrated how these messages affect listening; a person might hear and react to echoes from the past rather than the voice of the present. Recognizing these messages and their effects are part of the communication process.

As a person is able to recognize these messages and the effect that they have, he or she will be increasingly able to communicate from a space beyond the effect of those messages. In some cases, it may be possible to tell a person that the response is a reaction to "flashes from the past." In other cases, a person may need to be able to move his or her self to a space beyond those messages, or to adjust their reaction in a way that negates the power of the message. Again, the REBT process is an excellent way to deal with these situations.

If a person has learned to be afraid of their feelings, they may find it difficult to admit their feelings to themselves and to other people. This inability to face feelings can be a major hindrance for communication in relationships. If for instance, a person is afraid of being rejected, he or she may find it difficult to express his or her needs to another person. In order to avoid having to share needs and face rejection, they may suppress the need, trying to pretend that it isn't there. This denial does not eliminate that need; it will surface somehow. An unexpressed and unacknowledged need, however, often reveals itself in a less than desirable fashion. It is far better to learn to express one's feelings and needs than to repress them. An unexpressed need that reveals itself through inappropriate behavior causes problems that must then be discussed; the behavior adds to the problem.

People in recovery should also be aware that other people may have buried messages and that they may or may not be aware of them. If communication is a problem, they should look at interactions in the relationship to see if the other person is also reacting to something other than the current conversation. If so, let the nature of the relationship decide the reaction to the situation. In an intimate relationship, they may want to point out that the person seems to be reacting to something other than the present situation. In less intimate relationships, it may be necessary to make allowances for the person's actions.

There are techniques and skills that can be used to improve communication, some of which will be presented here. When people first start using them, they often report feeling uncomfortable. Clients should be encouraged to continue the use of these techniques, as they will become more automatic, and more comfortable, with practice.

One of the better-known techniques is the use of "I" statements; also called "I" messages. This is a way to express one's interests directly without evoking unnecessary defensiveness in the other person (Guilar, 2001). As an example, a person might feel frustrated that a significant other is not demonstrating a proper amount of trust. If that person says, "You hurt me when you don't trust me," then the significant other is likely to respond in a defensive manner. If, on the other hand, the person states, "I feel hurt that you don't trust me," then the door is left open for discussion rather than debate. This is simply a matter of accepting responsibility for one's own feelings and beliefs.

There are four components of an effective "I" message. First, as already stated, is ownership of the feeling or belief. The second is a statement of the problem. The third component is a statement of the intermediate goal; what the person would like to have happen. The final component is to express the reason for wanting this goal to be met (Guilar, 2001).

There are some things to keep in mind in using this tool. First, a proper "I" statement takes responsibility for feelings and beliefs. The statement, "I want you to stop hurting me," is not an effective "I" message, as it opens the door for argument as to whether or the person is actually being hurtful. On the other hand, stating, "I feel hurt by what you say, and I really don't like feeling that," would allow the person to then discuss what is hurtful and why the person perceives it in that manner.

I heard of a supervisor, who would say to her employees, "I'm going to give you an 'I' message." That statement negated any positive effect that the "I" message may have had. In making that announcement, the supervisor was implying that the person she was addressing was at fault. The supervisor also implied that she was going to be generous by giving that feedback in a nice manner, even though the other was in the wrong. Needless to say, that defeats the purpose of the technique.

Another effective technique is to confirm the other person's point of view. This does not mean that you have to agree with it; it is simply trying to see the situation as the other person sees it (Guilar, 2001). I have already discussed how attitudes and beliefs can affect communication. This is the process of trying to understand the point of view of the receiver. While this may not resolve the problem, it gives one a better chance of finding a solution. Knowing the backdrop of the other person's viewpoint can help in confirming that person's view. It is important to talk from your own point of view. Avoid saying things like, "You just think that..." or "You just wanted to..." as these statements assume knowledge of the other person's feelings and motives. Also, avoid saying things like, "I know how you feel." You may empathize with the person, but you cannot possibly know how they feel.

There are other ways to improve communication. One is to stay as positive as the situation permits. Avoid name-calling, sarcasm, threats, and intimidation. If you are talking about a behavior you don't like, attack the behavior, not the person. When possible, try to offer suggestions for solutions to a problem. Use the "sandwich" method when presenting information that could be perceived as negative; say something positive, offer the correction, then follow it with a positive statement. For example, you might say, "You have been very supportive of my recovery. I wish you could be more patient with my progress. I know you are doing your best to be understanding."

Another way to improve communication is by being clear and specific. Make your point clearly;

ask for what you want and tell how you feel. Avoid saying that a person "always" or "never" does something. If you are going to quote what someone said, be accurate; if you are talking about someone's actions, give specific times and examples. Avoid exaggeration, and stick to what is relevant.

It is also important to keep communication a two-way process. Don't monopolize; allow the other person a chance to respond while they can remember what is on their mind. Ask for feedback, for example, "Please tell me what you understood me to say." If the person did not understand, it allows you to rephrase the statement in a way that insures understanding.

Another aid to good communication is to stay on the subject. If possible, organize your thoughts ahead of time. Discuss one topic at a time and don't bring up issues that are already settled. Also, avoid "kitchen sinking," bringing up every problem and issue at one time.

Finally, good listening is an important part of communication. It is common to say, "I hear you." There is a big difference, however, between hearing and listening. Hearing is a physiological process of decoding sounds. Listening, on the other hand, is a process that involves four activities – selecting, attending, understanding, and remembering. These will lead to responding (Beebe, Beebe, and Redmond, 1999).

Selecting is the process of focusing on one sound out of the various sounds competing for attention. Sound is all around us; we are frequently unaware of many of the sounds. Yet, for effective communication, a person must choose to attend to the voice of the person that is speaking and try to filter out other sounds. Attending is focusing in on that sound. Attention can be fleeting, and people tend to focus on sounds that meet their needs or are consistent with what they think they should focus on. Attending is easier when a person feels they will be invited to participate or respond to what is being said.

Understanding is the process of assigning meaning to the sounds that are selected and attended to. I have already discussed ways that differences in culture and language can affect understanding. It is important for a person to assure that he or she understands the message that was given. One way to do this is for the listener to paraphrase what he understood the speaker to say, and to ask the speaker to confirm that the interpretation is correct. If it is not, then the speaker has the opportunity to clarify what was said. The final activity in listening is remembering. A person must remember what was said so that they may respond to it (Beebe, Beebe, and Redmond, 1999).

There are various modes of listening. There is active, or participatory, listening. This is an expressive form of listening. A person lets the speaker know they are listening through a variety of verbal and non-verbal cues. These include maintaining eye contact, focusing directly on the speaker, using facial expressions to show feelings and reactions, asking appropriate questions, and signaling understanding through phrases like "I see." To aid this process, a person should focus on the speaker, which is the process of selection that was discussed earlier. A person should also avoid the mistake of tuning out the speaker while planning his or her own next statement, or allowing the thoughts to stray to unrelated topics. A person should also assume that there is value in what the speaker has to say. This makes the listening process easier (DeVito, 1998).

It is important at times to understand what a person feels in order to understand what they mean; this is empathic listening. In order to do this, a person should view the speaker as an equal; try to understand both the thoughts and feelings, and to avoid prejudging what the speaker has to say. The listener tries to imagine his or her self in the place of the speaker.

I agree with Carl Rogers that communication is important, and that, in general, effective communication is not commonplace. Rogers states, "To understand another person's thoughts and feelings thoroughly, with the meanings they have for him, and to be thoroughly understood by this other person in return – this is one of the most rewarding of human experiences, and all too rare" (Rogers, 1961). Effective recovery is really nothing more than effective living, and good communication is one of the keys to achieve that.

Chapter Ten:
A Positive Approach to Relapse Prevention

The subject of relapse prevention and treatment is a major focus in the field of addiction counseling. Most insurance authorization forms ask if the client has developed a relapse prevention plan. Some treatment centers offer a special program for people who have relapsed after a period of sobriety. Terence Gorski, a well-known leader in the addiction field, has specialized in relapse prevention and treatment. His CENAPS® Corporation offers classes and special certification for Relapse Specialists.

While I recognize that relapse is a possibility in the recovery process, I also feel that the constant focus on relapse is not of benefit to clients. I find that a focus on "not failing" may actually set people up to fail in their recovery. I prefer to have clients focus on building and maintaining recovery; in doing this, they ultimately end up preventing relapse. I call this approach Success-Centered Addiction Recovery Facilitation. (SCARF)

In this chapter I define relapse and explore several theories of relapse. I also explore how Gorski and Ellis view relapse, and evaluate the strengths and weaknesses of those views. I then offer a new way to address relapse prevention and treatment. I will also discuss the need to convince clients that they need a solid plan once the medication is stopped.

In general, relapse is a return to use of alcohol and other drugs. Gorski defines it in this way:

> "Relapse is a process that occurs within the patient and manifests itself in a progressive pattern of behavior that reactivates the symptoms of a disease or creates related debilitating conditions in a person that has previously experienced remission from the illness" (Gorski & Miller, 1982).

Perhaps the most important element of this definition is the idea of relapse as a process. Gorski suggests that the actual use of the drug is the end of the process. Gorski also emphasizes that the process occurs within the patient. While it is typical for a person to blame the relapse on outside forces, Gorski states that relapse patterns are formed by "attitudes, values, and behavioral responses that occur inside the patient" (Gorski & Miller, 1982).

How much of a problem is relapse in addiction treatment? Gorski states that "many, if not most, return to the use of alcohol at least once after making an honest commitment to sobriety and pursuing a structured recovery program" (Gorski & Miller, 1982). I have seen many clients return for inpatient and outpatient treatment several times within a three-year period.

Gorski suggests that relapse prevention must begin in the early phases of recovery. According to Gorski, "Relapse is not a conscious choice, but the end result of a conscious, but progressive, sequence of warning signs (Gorski & Miller, 1982)." If a person is able to identify these signs, they can stop the relapse before it leads to the use of the substance.

Gorski has compiled a list of thirty-seven warning signs. I will not list all of the warning signs, but will look at a few of the more common ones as well as a few that seem harder to comprehend.

One sign is a return to the denial that first prevented a person from getting into treatment. The person begins to question the need for total abstinence and may decide that he or she is capable of controlling drug use. Another warning sign, according to Gorski, is an adamant commitment to sobriety. While this sounds as though it would be positive, Gorski states that a person can become so convinced that they will never use drugs again, that he or she stops pursuing a recovery program, thus becoming prone to relapse.

Another sign is tendencies toward loneliness. The person increases isolation and avoidance of interactions with others. Loss of constructive planning is another relapse warning sign. Gorski states wishful thinking begins to replace planning and effort.

Gorski differentiates between therapeutic and non-therapeutic relapses. A therapeutic relapse is defined as a relapse that increases the chances of full recovery because it points out the "undeniable fact" that the person is addicted and cannot drink or use drugs. This is usually a short-term problem with low consequences. A non-therapeutic relapse is one that makes recovery more difficult. This is usually of a long-term nature, but even a short-term relapse can be non-therapeutic if it results in more extreme consequences.

Gorski suggests the use of relapse prevention support groups as a tool in avoiding and recovering from relapse. In his book, *How to Start a Relapse Prevention Support Group,* Gorski outlines a suggested structure for these groups, the membership requirements, how the relapse prevention group differs from an AA meeting, the need for sponsors, as well as answering the question, "When is relapse prevention finished?" His answer to that question is that the problem never goes away. As he states in that section, "We suffer from a disease called alcoholism, not 'alcohol*was*m'" (Gorski, 1989).

Albert Ellis, in *When AA Doesn't Work For You: Rational Steps to Quitting Alcohol*, offers a different view of relapse. While he agrees with AA that recovery is a life-long process, he does not view addiction as a disease that is chronic and life-long. He states, "you can recover from substance abuse – after all, millions of people have done so. *But you can never recover from being human"* (Ellis & Velton, 1992).

Being human, Ellis states, is being fallible. He states that the beliefs that support addiction are not part of a disease; they are simply human nature. It is the escalation of wants and desires into demands and musts. He also points out that being human means having the ability to change and transform one's self. He warns that people often think being "normal," as in "not addicted," will mean ecstasy, or at least a better feeling than one had while addicted. Ellis states that a person must be ready to accept that life without the drug will consist of ups and downs that are, after all, normal. The key to preventing relapse, according to Ellis, is recognize the irrational messages that support continued drug use and to dispute them using the Rational-Emotive Behavior Therapy (REBT) techniques.

Ellis agrees with Gorski that drinking or drug use does not lead to relapse. He, like Gorski, states that the use of the drug is the end of the process. He also suggests signs of relapse; most of them regarding irrational thought and messages, often referred to as "stinking thinking" in the recovery field. If a person is able to recognize the resurgence of these irrational messages, they can stop the process before it leads to drug use.

Each approach has strengths and weaknesses. While Gorski's model of relapse as a process is helpful, I find that the emphasis on relapse in addiction treatment is, in my experience, often counter-productive. I would sometimes have a client enter my outpatient group after completing an inpatient stay. They might remain clean for several weeks, but then would test positive for drugs or alcohol. When the results were presented to them, the usual reply was, "They said in inpatient that addiction is a disease of relapse." This served as a justification to the client; they were simply following the course of the disease. I also feel that long-term attendance in a relapse prevention support group is counter-productive. It keeps the person's focus on fear of failure.

Not surprisingly, I find the most affinity with Albert Ellis' approach to relapse. I am a firm believer in the effect of attitudes and beliefs on feelings and behaviors. I also agree with Ellis, as well as with Gorski, that relapse is a process, and that one can learn to recognize the warning signs and to make changes to prevent relapse before it happens. I do, however, feel that there are more causes of relapse than attitudes and beliefs and feel that these also need to be examined.

After looking at these two approaches to relapse prevention, I have come to find an view of relapse prevention that is compatible with both 12-Step programs and medication assisted recovery. Both the Gorski and the Ellis approaches have an influence, but my approach is more than a sum of its parts.

To begin, I do not talk about relapse prevention. Gorski states, "Recovery and relapse are two sides of the same coin" (Gorski & Miller, 1982). I agree completely with this statement. That is why, in my approach, the emphasis is on building and maintaining recovery rather than preventing relapse. It is, after all, the same thing. Maintaining recovery, however, presents a positive goal as opposed to the negative goal of preventing relapse. If one concentrates on the possibility of failure, failure is always hovering nearby. On the other hand, focusing on a successful recovery helps to build and strengthen that recovery. I presented this view to a group of clients recently; one asked me to repeat it and requested that I write it for him. All were excited about focusing on building recovery as opposed to preventing relapse.

I had a client in group who stated that he "always" relapsed after 90 days of "clean time." He would come to group each time stating, "It's 79 days," then, "It's 85 days." Each time, you could hear the apprehension in his voice become more pronounced. He was so focused on relapse that he was not able to allow himself to focus on recovery. He was a prime candidate for the building and maintaining recovery approach.

I advise clients to identify barriers to recovery and plan to overcome them. This recognizes that there are recovery barriers, but offers the assurance that one can overcome those barriers. A lapse or slip *may* happen, but it is not an inevitable event. If a person does slip, he or she is encouraged to get right back on track and to evaluate the events leading to the slip to learn how to prevent further slips. The person is also encouraged to forgive him or herself for the slip rather than building up guilt and shame.

Anyone who has been in a drug treatment program will tell you, usually in a very mechanical manner, that to prevent relapse one should change "people, places, and things." They usually can't tell you how to go about doing so, or what to do about those people, places, and things that cannot be changed. This model suggests ways to deal with these issues.

Clients are to list those people in their lives who use mood-altering substances. They then list those who can be avoided or eliminated from their life. They then list those people who cannot be avoided, and are asked to consider ways of adjusting their relationship with those people to best support their recovery. They also need to list people who can support their recovery, because changing people is more than dropping negative people; it is adding positive people.

There are also places that people associate with drug or alcohol use. Being in these places can cause the person to return to using because they provide cues that will stimulate the desire for the drug. Clients are asked to list places that are associated with drug or alcohol use, and to decide which can and which cannot be avoided. They then plan what they can do to maintain recovery if they must be in one of these places. Again, they also list places that will support their recovery.

Things, in relapse prevention, are objects, sounds, smells, situations, feelings, and other items that are closely associated with drug use and can trigger the desire to use the substance. One client told me that he had to stop watching "The Sopranos" on television, because he always would get high while watching it. If he tried watching after starting his recovery program, the desire for drug use would become overwhelming. In this model, clients are asked to list the things that may trigger drug cravings and to determine ways to deal with them.

In this model, there is also recognition that attitudes and beliefs can be barriers to recovery. In this regard, it draws heavily upon the work of Albert Ellis. The previous chapter on REBT examines some attitudes and beliefs and suggests ways to deal with them. Some of these are a negative attitude toward sobriety, self-pity, placing blame on others, and a belief that recovery is too hard. Clients are asked to examine these and other attitudes and beliefs that they might have and are then encouraged to use the ABC methods of REBT to dispute these beliefs.

My focus on recovery retention as opposed to relapse prevention, and the tools that are provided in this model, offers clients the opportunity to make positive changes in their lives. It provides structure, support, hope, and fosters self-acceptance and self-esteem. It helps clients to see recovery as an ongoing process that will improve their quality of life.

Chapter Eleven:
The Transitioning Process

Most of the physicians who prescribe medications to assist recovery see these medications as a short-term intervention. While some see medications as a tool for maintaining recovery, the general view seems to be that medication is a good way to help the person become stable enough to develop the skills needed for long-term recovery without medication.

The timing for this transition needs to be a cooperative process. The prescriber obviously has a lead role in this; they are, after all, the ones with the most knowledge of the medication and what is required medically for the transition. Counselors have an important role in helping the physician evaluate the client's readiness to support recovery without medication. The client also has an important part to play, since they are the ones who need to go through the physical changes and make sure that their recovery continues.

In many cases, the prescriber may have a general rule for the length of time for medication. It may not always agree with our timeline or the client's. I have seen some people try to transition too soon; they have not yet developed the skills to maintain recovery without the medication. Other times the client may be afraid to let go of the security that the medication provides. The counselor's job is to help the client assess their readiness and to make good decisions regarding their care.

It is, perhaps, inevitable that we will not always agree with the physician on the correct timing of the client's transitioning. That is to be expected. There are ways that this can be handled that will not have a negative affect on the needed balance of the physician/counselor/client relationship.

First of all, any disagreement between the doctor and the counselor must be handled outside of the client's view. The client needs to feel that his or her treatment providers are a reliable team. We must also present our concerns in a rational way that presents solid backing for our concerns about the client's ability to succeed. Remember that our job description includes the ability to present goals in measurable terms. If we can do this, it is easier for the physician to weigh our input and to better respond to that input.

As I continue to work with doctors, I find that my interactions with them grow and improve. Many medical doctors are not used to working with counselors, and many counselors are not used to dealing with doctors. After time I find that we build mutual understanding and respect and there are fewer times that we disagree.

Addiction counselors have specialized knowledge and are professionals in our field. Doctors also have specialized knowledge and are professionals in their field. It can be easy to have ego clashes when two professionals have an overlap in treatment. Both must recognize that the needs of the patient overrule the need for the professionals to be "right."

Once the team decides on the right time for the client to move from medication, they must help the client to develop a continuing recovery plan. A lot of the responsibility for this rests with the counselor and the client.

The continuing recovery plan should include several things. First, the client should be able to identify his or her recovery tools. That "tool box" should contain a variety of resources that can meet a variety of situations. The client should be able to identify potential triggers for relapse and should have plans in place to deal with them. The client needs to have support in place and know who to contact in case of impending relapse.

The client and counselor should also set a period of time for continued sessions after the medication is discontinued. There should be a minimum number of sessions set with the understanding that the number could be extended if the client feels the need or desire to do so. It is important that the client be discouraged from discontinuing medication and counseling at the same time as that may increase the possibility of relapse.

The doctor may want to have some follow-up with the client after the medication is discontinued; that should be arranged between the client and the doctor.

Ultimately, the goal is for the client to be just as successful in the maintenance phase of recovery as he or she was in the action phase. This goal can be best met if the team of the client, counselor, and the physician is working together efficiently.

Chapter Twelve:
Medications for Mental Health

As I was ready to complete the first edition of this book, I read an article in the *Addiction Counselor* magazine that quite surprised me. While I knew that there were differences of opinion in the past about the use of medication for mental health issues for people in recovery, I felt that the issue had been resolved. It seems that the difference of opinion still exists; I would be remiss if I did not address this in this book as well.

So far, I have been talking about medications that have been developed specifically to treat addiction issues. There are, however, many people who have co-occurring disorders; an addiction plus a mental health disorder. These people must be treated for both. Since there is a shortage of people truly able to provide dual-diagnosis treatment we need to be able to work as efficiently with psychiatrists as we do physicians prescribing medication for recovery.

Historically, one reason for the concern of many addiction counselors in regard to psychiatric medications is the once held belief that treating a person's mental health disorder would eliminate the addiction issue. This view has been largely abandoned, but the memory of that time lingers on.

Another concern is the misdiagnosis of addiction problems as mental illnesses. A person who is using cocaine and going from the highs of the drug's effect to the low when it wears off could easily be diagnosed as being bipolar. Giving that person mood stabilizers would not resolve the issue.

Clearly this is another place where clients need a partnership between mental health and addiction professionals. If we combine our efforts we can help clients to meet goals and improve the quality of life.

In the past five years the bulk of my work has been in mental health clinics rather than addiction clinics. In these cases I was the "resident addiction specialist" and would work with clients who had addictive disorders as a primary diagnosis. I had the advantage of working closely with mental health counselors and prescribers for support in dealing with the mental health issues while I could offer them help and support them with clients who had substance abuse disorders as a secondary diagnosis. I found this relationship to be both quite enlightening for me and my colleagues and very beneficial for the clients.

Many of the newer medications that are available for treating mental disorders work at balancing brain chemistry and are not addictive. While it is true that these medications will not "cure" the client's addiction, they do help stabilize the client to allow the client to work on building recovery skills. It makes no sense to me to suggest that the use of these medications as prescribed should be discouraged. If it helps a person in their sobriety it is a good thing. Again, it isn't "the" path to recovery, but it is certainly a part of that path.

There are still some frequently prescribed medications that are addictive and are not the best choice for a client with an addiction problem. If we are willing to work with prescribers and the mental health counselors we can help them to determine the safest and most effective course of action to treat the person's mental health disorder.

It is time that we stop seeing psychiatry as an enemy and start to explore ways that we can work as a team to meet our mutual goal of helping people to improve their quality of life.

Chapter Thirteen:
Marijuana and Medication Assisted Recovery

In the past, use of marijuana would often lead to discharge from treatment in most treatment programs. This is rapidly changing, especially in MAR programs.

The attitude of the general public toward use of marijuana is rapidly changing. As I write this in January 2014, there are twenty states, plus the District of Columbia, that allow medical use of marijuana; two states, Washington and Colorado, have legalized marijuana for recreational use. While the use of marijuana is still illegal by Federal law, the current administration has made a policy decision to not enforce those Federal laws.

When you look at medical marijuana laws, it seems that marijuana is a miracle drug; the website of the United Patient's Group (http://www.unitedpatientsgroup.com/resources/ill nesses-treatable) lists more than 200 illnesses treatable with cannabis. These range from cancer to eczyma, PMS to PTSD, and chronic renal failure to rosacea. I don't know of any other drug that is that versatile.

While marijuana is probably not as benign or beneficial for all as proponents would suggest, neither is it a drug that turns the boy next door into a wild-eyed demon as depicted in the 1936 film, Reefer Madness. There are people who use cannabis to a point of dependence; on the other hand, not everyone who smokes pot goes on the harder drugs. This change in the view of marijuana has led many treatment programs to change their policies about marijuana use.

Medication Assisted Recovery is, at the core, a harm reduction approach to treatment. While total abstinence may be the goal preferred by most treatment professionals, the first goal of medication assisted treatment is usually to help the client reduce the risk of overdose, to help them move toward a lifestyle that is less damaging to their physical health and mental health, and one that allows them to better engage in daily life functions. The attitude of many prescribers is that they would rather have a patient who is smoking pot than one who is drinking to excess or abusing opiates. These providers are not condoning use of marijuana, but are accepting it as a lesser of two evils.

I tend to support providers in the decision to not discharge those who smoke marijuana. As I mentioned in the chapter on Motivational Interviewing, I have found it to be much more effective to meet the client where they are at when they enter treatment, then use the skills I have, along with a strong therapeutic alliance, to move them to the place that will allow them to live a quality life.

Chapter Fourteen:
Closing Thoughts

Almost 50 years ago, Bob Dylan told us all that "The times they are a changing." Half a century later this still holds true. As important as tradition may be, it is also imperative that we recognize and embrace innovations that help us as we help our clients to meet their goals.

I have a great respect for the work of the founders of the addiction treatment field; they spent their lives trying to help those that many felt were helpless and hopeless. These founders set the stage for a new understanding of addiction and ways to treat the addiction.

In the time since then, however, there have been technological advancements that need to be seen as having the potential to improve as well and hinder addiction treatment.

The internet has certainly made it easier for people to learn about new ways to get high and find new addictions. At the same time it has made it easier for people to find local meetings and even develop "virtual" support systems. I have an increasing number of people calling for services who found me through internet searches.

In the same way, medication to assist the recovery process has come a long way. One hundred years ago there were "remedies" that were often more dangerous than the condition they were purported to cure. While we may lack research on the long-term effects of some of the medications used today we can be sure that they have been more carefully tested than those available in the past. To reject these medications based on past experiences would be a disservice to those we want to help.

We don't have to, as Jack Trimpey once urged, take sides. We can work together to improve the lives of those caught in the web of addiction. If you find the approach that works for *you* and is best for *your* clients, that is good. If you can also accept that other professionals have different ways to treat addiction, and that clients have many different needs that require different approaches, we are one step closer to making success in recovery a reality for all.

Appendix A
The Eight Principles of Positive Path Recovery

A number of the techniques that I have discussed in this book are part of my Positive Path Recovery approach. I felt that it would be good to present an overview of the Eight Principle of Positive Path Recovery and some of the worksheets realated to the approach here. If you want more information, I present more detail in my book, *Positive Path Recovery..*

Positive Path Recovery was developed in my early years of practice. As I explored the literature and worked with clients, I began to recognize specific areas that seemed to be common to most people with addiction problems. Over a period of time, these observations developed into specific treatment goals and actions. Eventually, I distilled this into Eight Principles that form the basis for Positive Path Recovery. These Principles are:

1) Admit that the substance has taken control and commit to a path of recovery.
2) Redefine and rebuild the sense of self. (The true self)
3) Take responsibility and accept forgiveness for past actions.
4) Learn to identify and express feelings.
5) Improve communication with others.
6) Restore connection with significant people and make connection with others who can support recovery.

7) Identify barriers to recovery and plan to overcome them.
8) Let Go!

These Principles are ongoing tasks rather than progressive steps. While I feel that there are certain techniques that will aid the client in these tasks, I do not impose a rigid structure on the client. I consider the client's experiences, beliefs, goals, and needs to determine the best method to treat the client.

The book, *PositivePath Recovery,* offers in-depth looks at some of the theory and techniques behind these Principles, but for now I will give a brief overview of each.

Principle One uses elements of Reality Therapy to help the client recognize that the chemical use is not solving their problem and is, most likely, making things worse. It then uses the Stages of Change model and Motivational Interviewing approaches to aid in the commitment process.

For Principle Two, there are a series of questions that are used to help the person discover the true self. This includes questions about self-image, beliefs about the world, moral and ethical guidelines, wants, needs, and goals. Guided visualization is also used to help a client look deeper within. Appendices B and C offer techniques to aid this process.

Principle Three, taking responsibility for past actions, is another example of the use of Reality Therapy. This involves recognizing the effect that substance use had on the client and the client's friends, family, and work or school environment. Another part of this task is to accept forgiveness. This includes self-forgiveness, recognizing that excessive guilt and shame can lead to continued or renewed, substance use.

Principle Four, learning to identify and express feelings, has its roots in Cognitive/Behavioral theory. Since that model suggests that feelings are based on beliefs, one must first be able to identify feelings that are affecting behavior in order to discover the beliefs behind the feelings. Ellis' REBT is a major component of this task; it is covered in more detail in Chapter Eight of this book.

Improving communication is, perhaps, not as deeply based in psychological theory as it is in basic communication theory. Some of the techniques offered to the client, however, are found in Carl Rogers' Person Centered Therapy. The need for communication skills and information on building them is covered in Chapter Nine.

Principle Six, restoring connection with significant people, has its roots in Family Systems Theory. One must make an effort to restore balance to the family. Additionally, there is a need for the support of substance-free individuals. In my model, these do not have to be recovering substance abusers, although the use of AA and NA is encouraged, as there are benefits from sharing the experience of others who have faced similar problems. Additional forms of support may be SMART Recovery groups, sober friends, co-workers, or others in the person's treatment program.

Principle Seven, identifying barriers to recovery and planning to overcome them, is, in the common terminology of addiction treatment, relapse prevention. The basics of relapse prevention, as commonly taught, are to change people, places, and things. In Positive Path Recovery, I also stress the need to change attitudes and beliefs; this is firmly rooted in the Cognitive/Behavioral model, especially in the work of Albert Ellis and Jack Trimpey. An emphasis is also made on viewing this as building recovery rather than preventing relapse. This is discussed further in Chapter Ten.

The final Principle of the Positive Path approach, letting go, is simply learning to move from the past. A basic tool of twelve-step treatment, the Serenity Prayer, states that a person needs to accept what they can't change, change what they can, and to understand the difference. There is great wisdom in this. If a client tries too hard to change things that are beyond their control, the risk of frustration leading to relapse is increased. Learning to change what can be changed, such as the way a person responds to an event, can move a person along in their recovery.

The Positive Path Recovery approach is not presented as "the way" to treat addiction. It is, instead, presented as "a way" to do so. It recognizes that there are many people who have responded well to the twelve-step model of treatment. At the same time, it recognizes that there are also many who have not responded to that model and offers an alternative approach for those people.

This model can be used for anyone presenting for addiction treatment, but I feel there are some groups of people for whom this approach is especially indicated. One group would be people with one or more unsuccessful attempts at recovery through the twelve-step model. Addiction professionals often tell their clients that insanity is "doing the same thing repeatedly, expecting different results." At the same time, these professionals will offer the same treatment approach time after time. The Positive Path program offers the client a new way to approach recovery.

Another group of people who may benefit from this approach are those with strong feelings against spirituality and anything that may be perceived as "religious." There are many people who object to the "God talk" of the twelve-step model; these objections prevent them from gaining the benefit of treatment. Others may have spiritual beliefs, but find the twelve-step approach too rigidly Judeo/Christian for their comfort. It should be noted that the Positive Path is not opposed to spirituality. It does, however, recognize that spiritual belief and understanding is a very personal thing. As a result, it avoids reference to terms associated with spirituality.

People who are highly rational or self-directed may also have problems with the highly directive approach of the twelve steps. While it is true that a person in addiction probably has a history of making poor choices, it does not necessarily follow that they are incapable of making better choices. I remember hearing a co-worker once tell a client that they should not think for the first year of recovery. While I appreciate what this counselor was trying to say, I can see that it would be very difficult advice to follow. The Positive Path approach teaches the person how to make healthier choices.

Positive Path Recovery is another tool that is available to the treatment professional and to the person in recovery. It should not be viewed as an attempt to undermine any present form of treatment; it is designed to expand and compliment the methods that are available in the field of substance abuse treatment.

Appendix B
Guided Visualization for Connecting to the True Self

Guided visualization is a technique that can help to reconnect a person with the true self. The following visualization is a centering exercise that allows a person to imagine his or her self making a journey into the deeper recesses of the self. Playing quiet, relaxing music can help to make this exercise more effective. For self-directed visualization, it would be best to record the exercise ahead of time. I have indicated spaces where you may want to pause to allow time for reflection and revelation.

Close your eyes, find a comfortable position, and begin to connect with the pattern of your breathing. (Pause) As you breathe in and out, imagine that the rhythm of your breathing is the rhythm of life. (Pause) Imagine that you are standing at the beginning of a path that leads into a deep forest, The sun is shining down through the trees, creating a pattern of light and shadow on the grassy path ahead. (Pause) At the end of the path, you can see a bright light; this is the light of the sun illuminating a beautiful garden that is in the center of the woods. (Pause) As you continue to connect with your breath, the Earth's heartbeat, begin to travel down the path, taking time to notice the beauty that surrounds you. (Pause) As you travel this path, you hear the sound of a rippling stream, distant at first, but becoming louder as you continue walking. (Pause) As you travel this path, appreciating the beauty that surrounds you, you may find obstacles that impede your progress. Take note of these obstacles, knowing that they may slow your journey; you also know that they will not prevent you from continuing on the path to your destination. (Pause) After you have identified these obstacles, move past them and continue down the path, realizing that the encountering and bypassing the obstacle has brought you closer to the clearing at the center of the forest. (Pause) You slowly approach that clearing; the warmth of the sunlight brings a sense of comfort and connection to your heart and soul. Relax in the sunlight, rejoicing in its restorative power. (Pause) Kneel at the side of the stream; notice how clear and soothing the water is. (Pause) As you look into the stream, you see a reflection of yourself; this reflection shows the beauty that is reflected from your depth. (Pause) You sit by the stream, looking at the reflection; you are filled by the warmth of the sun and by the knowledge and awareness of your inner beauty. (Pause) When you are ready, slowly move back to the path, returning to the place where you began this trip. (Pause) As you continue your return trip, you will once again pass the obstacles that you encountered earlier; make note of them, knowing that they are not as powerful now as they were when you first encountered them. (Pause) As you approach the head of the path, you once again become aware of the pattern of your breathing. (Pause) Very slowly and gently open your eyes, allowing yourself to return to the present reality.

Appendix C
Redefining and Restoring the True Self

The following questions will help you to identify your true self. Allow yourself time to give thoughtful answers to these questions.

What do I believe about myself?

What do I believe about others?

What do I believe about the world around me?

What is important to me?

What moral or ethical guidelines do I feel that I must follow?

What must I have in order to feel fulfilled and at peace?

What do I want from life for myself and for others?

What are my strengths?

What are my weaknesses?

Appendix D
Relationships

Take some time to consider the people who are involved in your life. Some will help to build recovery; some will hurt recovery, while others will support recovery in an indirect manner.

Relationships that are important to my recovery:

Relationships I would like to continue if possible:

Relationships that can hurt my recovery:

Relationships that I would like to form, to support my recovery:

Appendix E
Identifying and Overcoming Recovery Barriers

Part of building recovery is recognizing possible barriers to recovery and planning to overcome those barriers. Common barriers are people, places, things, attitudes and beliefs. The following exercise will help to identify barriers as well as ways to deal with them.

List all people who use mood-altering substances and who play a significant role in your life:

List those who can be avoided or eliminated from your life:

List those who you cannot avoid or eliminate:

How can you adjust your relationship with them to prevent them from undermining your recovery?

What people can you add to support recovery?

What places do you associate with alcohol or drug use?

Which of these places can you easily stay away from?

Which of these places can not be avoided?

What can you do to maintain your recovery while you are in these places?

What places would support recovery?

What situations usually accompanied drug use?

Are there sights, sounds, or other things that make you think of drugs?

Choose several of these and develop ways to deal with them. (Avoidance, building new associations or reactions, etc.)

What is an attitude or belief that might block your recovery?

How can you dispute that attitude or belief?

What is another attitude or belief that might block your recovery?

How can you dispute that attitude or belief?

Bibliography

Alcoholics Anonymous World Services, Inc. (1976). *Alcoholics Anonymous*. New York: Author

American Psychiatric Association. (2000). *Diagnostic and Statistical Manual of Mental Disorders (Fourth Edition) Text Revision – DSM-IV- TR*. Washington, DC: Author

Beebe, S., Beebe, S., & Redmond, M. (1999) *Interpersonal Communication: Relating to Others*. Boston: Allyn & Bacon.

Corey, G. (1981). *Theory and Practice of Group Counseling*. Monterey, CA: Brooks/Cole Publishing Company.

DeVito, J. (1998). *The Interpersonal Communication Book*. New York: Longman

Ellis, A. & Harper, R. (1975). *A New Guide to Rational Living*. N. Hollywood: Wilshire Book Company.

Ellis, A., McInerney, J.F., DiGiuseppe, R., & Yeager, R.J. (1988). *Rational-Emotive Therapy with Alcoholics and Substance Abusers*. Boston: Allyn & Bacon.

Ellis, A. & Velton, E. (1992). *When AA Doesn't Work for You: Rational Steps to Quitting Alcohol*. Fort Lee, NJ: Barricade Books.

Fiorentine, R., & Anglin, M. (1997). Does Increasing the Opportunity for Counseling Increase the Effectiveness of Outpatient Drug Treatment? *American Journal of Drug and Alcohol Abuse 23*, 369-383. (Download from Norwich University Expanded Academic ASAP.)

Firman, J. & Gila, A. (1997). *The Primal Wound: A Transpersonal View of Trauma, Addiction, and Growth*. Albany: State University of New York Press.

Glasser, W. (1965). *Reality Therapy: A New Approach to Psychiatry*. New York: Harper and Row

Gorski, T. (1989). *How to Start Relapse Prevention Support Groups*. Independence, MO: Herald House/Independence Press.

Gorski, T. & Miller, M. (1982). *Counseling for Relapse Prevention.* Independence, MO: Herald House/Independence Press.

Grof, C. (1993). *The Thirst for Wholeness: Attachment, Addiction, and the Spiritual Path*. New York: HarperCollins Publisher.

Guilar, J. (2001). *The Interpersonal Communications Skill Workshop: A Trainer's Guide*. New York: American Management Association.

Kuhn, C., Swartzwelder, S., & Wilson, W. (1998). *Buzzed: The Straight Facts About the Most Used and Abused Drugs from Alcohol to Ecstasy.* New York: W. W. Norton & Company.

Miller, W et al (1999). *Enhancing Motivation for Change in Substance Abuse Treatment.* Washington, DC: SAMSHA

Mueller, L. & Ketcham, K. (1987). *Recovering: How to Get and Stay Sober.* New York: Bantam Books

Nakken, C. (1988). *The Addictive Personality: Understanding Compulsion in Our Lives.* New York: HarperCollins Publisher.

National Institute on Drug Abuse (NIDA). (2000). *Principles of Drug Addiction Treatment: A Research Based Guide.* Washington, D.C.: Author

O'Brien, C. (1997). A Range of Research-Based Pharmacotherapies for Addiction. *Science, 278*(5335), 66-71. (Download from Norwich University Expanded Academic ASAP.)

Pita, D. (1992). *Addictions Counseling.* New York: Crossroad Publishing

Rogers, C. (1961). *On Becoming a Person.* Boston: Houghton Mifflin Company

Sawrey, J. & Telford, C. (1971). *Psychology of Adjustment.* Boston: Allyn and Bacon

Scott, C (2000). Ethical Issues in Addiction Counseling. *Rehabilitation Counseling Bulletin 43*, 209 – 215. (Download from Norwich University Expanded Academic ASAP.)

Shulman, L. (1992). *The Skills of Helping: Individuals, Families, and Groups* (3rd Ed.), Itasca, IL: F.E. Peacock Publishers, Inc.

Stewart, J. (Ed.). (1999). *Bridges Not Walls: A Book About Interpersonal Communication* (7th Ed.). Boston: McGraw-Hill College.

Substance Abuse and Mental Health Services Administration. (1999) *Brief Interventions and Brief Therapies for Substance Abuse.* Rockville, MD: Author

Thombs, D. (1994). *Introduction to Addictive Behaviors.* New York: The Guilford Press

Trimpey, J. (1989). *The Small Book.* New York: Delacorte Press

Trimpey, J. (1996). *Rational Recovery: The New Cure for Substance Addiction.* New York: Pocket Books

Walant, K. (1995). *Creating the Capacity for Attachment: Treating Addictions and the Alienanted Self.* Northvale, N.J.: Jason Aronson Inc.

White, W (2001, April). A Disease Concept for the 21st Century. *Counselor: The Magazine for Addiction Professionals, 2,* pp.48-52.

White, W & Miller W (2007, August) The Use of Confrontation in Addiction Treatment. *Counselor: The Magazine for Addiction Professionals, 4,* pp.12-30.

Winger, G., Hofmann, F., & Woods, J. (1992). *A Handbook on Drug and Alcohol Abuse: The Biomedical Aspects.* New York, NY: Oxford University Press.

Yalom, I. (1995). *The Theory and Practice of Group Psychotherapy.* (Fourth Edition). New York: Basic Books

Other Resources

Websites:

www.naadac.org – NAADAC, the Association for Addiction Professionals, represents the professional interests of more than 75,000 addiction counselors, educators and other addiction-focused health care professionals in the United States, Canada and abroad. NAADAC's members are addiction counselors, educators and other addiction-focused health care professionals, who specialize in addiction prevention, treatment, recovery support and education. An important part of the healthcare continuum, NAADAC members and its 44 state affiliates work to create healthier individuals, families and communities through prevention, intervention, quality treatment and recovery support.

www.samhsa.gov - The Substance Abuse and Mental Health Services Administration (SAMHSA) is the agency within the U.S. Department of Health and Human Services that leads public health efforts to advance the behavioral health of the nation. SAMHSA's mission is to reduce the impact of substance abuse and mental illness on America's communities. The site has a lot of good information, including an on-line treatment locator and a lot of free books and other information. They have an excellent Anger Management program with books for the group leader as well as for participants that is designed for addicted clients.

www.aatod.org - The American Association for the Treatment of Opioid Dependence (AATOD) was founded in 1984 to enhance the quality of patient care in treatment programs by promoting the growth and development of comprehensive opioid treatment services throughout the United States. This site offers many useful resources for counselors.

www.suboxone.com - This site offers information for patients, prescribers, and therapists. It includes a search program that allows patients to find prescribers in their area; this is helpful for counselors who want to connect with their local doctors.

www.vivitrol.com – On this site you can find information about the use of Vivitrol for alcohol dependence and opiate dependence. There is a section for health professionals that offers a lot of useful information.

www.motivationalinterview.org - This site is the best resource for information on MI. The materials included here are designed to facilitate the dissemination, adoption and implementation of MI among clinicians, supervisors, program managers and trainers, and improve treatment outcomes for clients with substance use disorders.

www.positivepathcounseling.org – This is the webpage for my counseling practice, but there is also information about Positive Path Recovery there. There is also contact information; I am always willing to offer information and answer questions.

About The Author

Gary Blanchard began his career in the addiction treatment field after graduation from College of Notre Dame of Maryland's Weekend College in 1998. In 2000, Gary enrolled in Vermont College of Norwich University; he received a Masters in Addictions Counseling from Vermont College in 2002.

Since moving to West Brookfield, Massachusetts, in 2006, Gary worked in programs for people with co-occurring disorders. He also has a private practice, providing counseling in Ware, Massachusetts. Gary teaches at Holyoke Community College in Holyoke, Massachusetts. He is a licensed alcohol and drug counselor; in 2014 he was named Counselor of the Year by the Massachusetts Association of Alcohol and Drug Abuse Counselors (MAADAC).

Gary is the author of *Positive Path Recovery* and *How to Build and Maintain Recovery.* He has presented at many local and national conferences. He is currently the President of MAADAC.

Made in the USA
Coppell, TX
12 April 2020

19824360R00075